Lullaby of Broadway

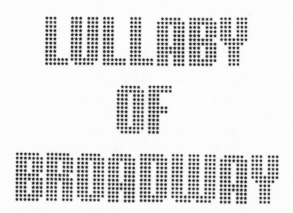

LULLABY
OF
BROADWAY

Patricia Dubin McGuire

CITADEL PRESS   SECAUCUS, NEW JERSEY

Published by Citadel Press
A division of Lyle Stuart Inc.
120 Enterprise Avenue, Secaucus, N.J. 07094
In Canada: Musson Book Company,
A division of General Publishing Co. Limited
Don Mills, Ontario

Queries regarding rights and permissions should be
addressed to: Lyle Stuart Inc., 120 Enterprise Avenue,
Secaucus, N.J. 07094

Manufactured in the United States of America

Library of Congress Cataloging in Publication Data

McGuire, Patricia Dubin, 1922–
    Lullaby of Broadway.

    1. Dubin, Al.   2. Librettists—United States—
Biography.   I. title.
ML423.D74M3 1983 782.81′092′4 [B] 83-7690
ISBN 0-8065-0871-X

To Al Dubin's three grandchildren—who
never had the pleasure of knowing the man
in the flesh—Loddy, Annie and Greg, this
book is lovingly dedicated.

PROLOGUE

WHO COULD WRITE a history of the thirties in America and leave out the popular song? We still whistle, hum and sing the songs of the thirties while many of the men who wrote those songs have been forgotten. Though the authors and composers of the era made a major contribution in terms of helping people cope with economic depression, that contribution is often discounted as frivolous. But life is made up of frivolity, detail, trivia, "everydayness." Which of us has not sung in the shower to prepare for a new day? Songs people sing often tell historians as much about the times and the culture as books they read, food they eat, clothes they wear, idols they worship.

In the 17th century, Shakespeare gave us two gentlemen from Verona; in the 1930's Warner Brothers gave us two gentlemen from Manhattan—Al Dubin and Harry Warren, songwriters extraordinaire.

Al Dubin was my father.

The man who wrote the whimsical "Tiptoe Through the Tulips," the nostalgic "Indian Summer," the swinging "Lulu's Back in Town" and the Academy Award-winning "Lullaby of Broadway" lived a chaotic life, filled with wild escapades and extravagant excesses, ending at the age of fifty-three in a New York City hospital with only strangers by his bedside.

As I sat on opening night at the Winter Garden Theatre on Broadway in August of 1980 enjoying David Merrick's production of *Forty-Second Street,* I marvelled at the reception the audience gave to the songs of Warren and Dubin, written over forty years ago in the Depression era. The audience responded with instant and joyful recognition to the songs, but who, I reflected, remembered the fat man who gave birth to those lyrics, or the sunny Italian gentleman from Brooklyn who composed the music? A very select few.

So this is a memoir of Al Dubin, thoughtfully researched, with an honest attempt to put facts in an objective manner. But colored by time, by others' viewpoints, by the subjectivity of a daughter—and by love.

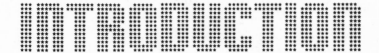

INTRODUCTION

I FIRST MET Al Dubin at the Oyster Bar in Grand Central Station in New York. I love oysters and so did he. We started to talk, first about food, and then we discovered we were in the same business. We were both songwriters.

Al was an excellent conversationalist with an extensive vocabulary—a good trait for a lyricist to have. I liked Al from that first meeting and enjoyed his wry sense of humor. We wrote a couple of songs together and he was a guest in my home in Forest Hills on a few occasions.

Al came to Hollywood before I did. He worked with several composers but, principally, with Joe Burke. The first song Al and I wrote together out here at Warner Brothers was a song called "Too Many Tears." My tune was an off-beat tango, difficult to put a lyric to, but Al did a great job. It wasn't long after that we were assigned to do the score for *Forty-Second Street*.

We worked very hard on that score and spent crazy days and nights working with "Buzz" Berkeley, Ray Heindorf, Lloyd Bacon. Al and I used to call "Buzz" "The Madman."

9

Working with Al was never dull. He disappeared a lot, but he always came through with those lyrics. In my opinion, he was a great lyric writer, one of the greatest. Time has proven that. He not only was a lyricist for his time and place, but a whole new generation still sings his songs—songs like "Forty-Second Street," "You're Getting to Be a Habit with Me," "I Only Have Eyes for You," "Lullaby of Broadway." Al told me he wrote "Lullaby of Broadway" for me because in those days I missed New York so much.

Al was a warm, friendly man who knew how to have a good time. He might have stained our office wall a few times with tobacco juice when he missed the cuspidor, but I never heard him say a critical thing about a fellow-lyricist. The big man was a strange combination of naïveté and sophistication. He was versatile. He could write a wildly sentimental ballad like "I'll Sing You a Thousand Love Songs," a song of social protest like "Remember My Forgotten Man," or a clever, humorous number like "She's a Latin from Manhattan."

Al was a very sensitive man. If you criticized his lyrics, he got very hurt. But you didn't criticize his lyrics often. You didn't have to. He was too good.

When he left Warner Brothers to work on Broadway shows in New York, I was sad to see him go. We had worked together so intensely and so well. We had a kind of magic chemistry going between us when we wrote. Neither one of us really understood it.

Al played a big part in my professional Hollywood life. He was an inspiration to me. Quite simply, without Al Dubin, it never could have happened.

Harry Warren
April, 1980
Beverly Hills, Calif.

Lullaby of Broadway

ONE

"GOOD EVENING, Mr. and Mrs. America, from border to border and coast to coast and all the ships at sea. Let's go to press!"

The familiar, sharp, staccato sound of Walter Winchell's voice reached across the airwaves and into the den of our Beverly Hills home as my mother and I carried in our dinner trays. Listening to the famed radio broadcaster and news columnist had become a ritual in countless Southern California households and ours was no exception.

The next words came so fast, startling both of us. We did not hear them all but we did hear ". . . Al Dubin—lyricist of Academy Award-winning "Lullaby of Broadway"—dead—age fifty-three—Roosevelt Hospital—New York City."

My mother and I stared, unbelieving, at one another. Had Winchell said "dead"? Perhaps "dying"? We both

needed and dreaded confirmation. Al Dubin was her husband, my father.

The terrible message was confirmed for me when I called Harry Warren, his long-time collaborator.

Yes, he had heard. And with that, Harry started to cry. My tears followed as the pain of reality replaced the numbness of disbelief. My father's life was really over. Done with. Finis!

The date was February 11, 1945.

The Jewish boy from Philadelphia who was given the last rites of the Catholic Church before he died, lost out to pneumonia and barbiturate poisoning, ending his former brilliant career as a Hollywood musical lyricist, and ending, too, his faltering career in New York. His death put an end to his chaotic life of compulsions and broken dreams.

The life that ended on that fine February day had begun in Zurich, Switzerland, on June 10, 1891. Al Dubin was the firstborn son of Simon and Minna Dubin. Simon had fled Russia to continue his medical studies at Berne University in Switzerland, where he met Minna, who taught classes in analytical chemistry. Though Simon and Minna were both Eastern European Jews, they embraced a philosophy of "ethical culture," rejecting the traditional concept of God in favor of an intellectual agnosticism. In addition, both of them were militantly anti-Czarist.

Simon's parents, Marcus and Ida, had tried to dissuade the young man from leaving home, but he felt life was not worth living with the total lack of freedom that existed in 19th century Russia.

So these two young people had much in common when they met in Berne. Simon asked Minna to marry

him, and though she had not intended to become any-one's wife, Minna decided that Simon was not "anyone," but shared her philosophy so completely it was as if he were but another part of her. So the two of them married on June 6, 1890.

Minna had decided in her early teens that she did not want to raise children; it would certainly interfere with her life as a scientist, to which she was so totally committed. But Simon confided in his new bride that he wanted a son. He argued that a child of theirs, son or daughter, would most certainly be bright, would probably be talented and would surely make a contribution to society. Minna was convinced by the arguments and agreed to bear a child.

On June 10, 1891, Minna gave birth to an eight-pound, nine-ounce son. Typical of any new mother, she was enchanted with her green-eyed, sandy-haired baby, whom she promptly named Alexander, after Alexander the Great, who had conquered the world before his thirtieth birthday. Minna was convinced that this was no ordinary child and marvelled that he could hold his head up when he was barely two weeks old.

Six weeks after Alexander's birth, Minna returned to her teaching post, hiring Hildy, a young Swiss girl from the neighboring mountains, to look after her son. Simon argued with his wife about nursing the baby, telling Minna that cow's milk was not safe for such a young child—cows carried tuberculosis and other life-threatening germs. But Minna would not defer to Simon, telling him she could not teach her class and nurse a child. So Simon purchased a goat from Hildy's father and Hildy milked the animal to insure a safe and steady supply for little Alick, as they called him.

The Dubins celebrated Alick's first birthday with a special dinner with friends and colleagues, and were grateful that their son was healthy, active and curious. But such curiosity and energetic enthusiasm presented a problem to Minna on the rare days when Hildy was ill and did not come to care for the little boy. Simon was distressed that Minna tied her son to the crib so she would not miss her class. Little Alick fought the ropes to no avail, and began about this time to suffer from nightmares.

Though Minna Dubin, preoccupied as she was with her life of science and teaching, was hardly the prototype of a 19th century housewife, she and Simon gathered about them a closely knit circle of friends who shared many of their political convictions. The Dubins and their nihilist friends talked about the United States and what it had to offer. Did one have to be enormously rich to live there; could Minna learn to speak English well enough so she could pursue her career? (Simon already knew the language.) What were the opportunities? From all they learned from others they began to fantasize about a land of limitless opportunities; of a country where prejudice did not exist; a creative, vigorous new world where their beliefs would be respected; where they could truly be who they were.

In earnest they investigated the various cities to discover which one would afford Simon the best opportunity to practice medicine. Their research told them that Philadelphia was a medical-surgical center, that its first hospital, the Pennsylvania, had been chartered in 1751. The first school of anatomy there had been established in 1762, and the first Medical College in 1765. There was a College of Pharmacy; Jefferson Medical College;

Women's Medical College; Hahnemann Medical College. In addition, there was a relatively new college called Gratz which had been founded in 1893 for the purpose of furthering and fostering Hebrew learning.

Simon discovered that Philadelphia had set up the first free library in the American colonies, which was called the Loganian; it was founded in 1745 and opened to an eager public in 1760. Also, the first subscription library, founded by Benjamin Franklin, was to be found in Philadelphia. In short, the city was the cultural center of the country and was also in the process of becoming a great industrial showplace.

This contrast to their native Russia excited both Simon and Minna, who decided this was where they wanted to start a new life. This was the place they wanted to raise their son. Alick would grow up in a land of opportunity where there was freedom and justice for all—including Jews; where pogroms did not exist; where there were no reprisals for differing beliefs or lifestyles from an oppressive ruling class.

So when Alick was five years old, they packed up their belongings, said goodbye to their colleagues and students at Berne University, travelled by train from Switzerland to Germany and set sail from Bremen, arriving in the Port of Philadelphia in the summer of 1896.

As Minna and Simon stood on deck of the ship as it glided into port, holding their small son, they were a happy and expectant young couple, dreaming dreams of their own success in this city that boasted a population of one million people. And dreaming, too, of that future time when little Alick would enter one of the fine medical schools in the United States.

"He already has the hands of a fine surgeon," his father would proudly declare, even when the boy was very small.

"Perhaps he shall grow up to be a chemist and make an important medical discovery," his mother would say. "After all, it is the chemists who give the doctors the tools with which to cure people."

Though there was much competition and some disagreement between Simon and Minna, they were agreed that Alick, like them, would surely devote his life to science.

When they were settled, Simon set up a practice in the family home at 325 Pine Street and by 1900 was the Gynecology Chief of the Dispensary Staff of Mt. Sinai Hospital, now called Albert Einstein Medical Center. Simon also became one of a small but vocal group of doctors who worked towards medical upgrading in the care of immigrants while fighting against unacceptable medical standards of the time.

Minna, meanwhile, a reluctant but indulgent mother, hired a young Polish girl named Mary to look after her son. Though Minna spoke no English, she still hoped to find a position as a chemist. When it proved out of the question, she went to work as a seamstresss—whether to help a struggling Simon pay the bills or whether sewing in a factory proved more attractive than domesticity is hard to tell. Maybe both reasons determined the choice.

A tiny (four feet, eleven inches tall) but physically strong woman, Minna sewed buttons by day and attended school in the evenings to learn English. Eventually, she was introduced to Dr. Herman Schanche, a native of Norway who had been educated in Germany. Minna, who spoke German as well as Russian, was given

a job as chemist at Harrison Brothers and Co., Inc., located at 35th and Grays Ferry Road. The company was eventually purchased by Dupont Chemical Company.

Yiddish, Russian and German were the languages spoken in the home, but Alick still made his requests in a Swiss mountain dialect he had learned in Zurich from his nursemaid Hildy. So he was rather unprepared when it was time for him to start school.

His parents enrolled him in a public elementary school and Alick felt shy and strange. Bewildered by new customs and with no English in his vocabulary, he panicked when he had to use the bathroom and did the only thing he could think to do—indicated with gestures to a group of boys what his problem was. One of the boys, a bit older and a whole lot more sophisticated than Alick, picked up a stone and threw it, pointing and nodding that where the stone landed was, indeed, the toilet. It was. The girls' toilet. Though he laughed about the incident in adult life, Al never quite forgot the small boy's humiliation at having been betrayed.

As he grew into boyhood, as he learned the language, he was no longer tied to a bed with a long rope as he had been in Zurich. Now he was given unlimited freedom by his two busy parents. He could eat when and what he wanted, sleep when he felt in the mood, stay with his friends at his own discretion. He interpreted this freedom as he had the restriction of being tied to the bed, as a lack of caring. He lied often to his peers, telling them he had to be home by six o'clock or he would "catch hell." He wanted to be one of those regular people whose parents set up strict rules and guidelines. Al wanted to be accepted as one of the guys.

He possessed all the attributes—he was attractive with an excellent physique; was quick, alert, bright and, most important for a boy who wants to belong, he was a well-above-average athlete. But, in spite of all he had going for him in those very early days, Al could not shake the feeling that he was marching to a different drummer.

When Al was not quite ten years old, his mother, much to her chagrin, bore another son, whom she named Joseph. Joseph was not planned for and Minna's unhappiness at being burdened with another child to care for was not lost on the sensitive Al. While he longed for a tender mother who baked cookies, he got a cool mother who talked of chemical equations.

Minna's concern over the birth of her second son grew partially out of her own childhood disillusionments. The daughter of a wealthy Russian merchant, she had been one of the youngest of eleven children. As a child, she watched, horrified, as her father came home with five or six friends and demanded that food and drink be served by his wife. Minna told Alick she remembered one painful occasion when her mother had given birth to a child only four days earlier, but had to wait on the men even though she was still weak from the delivery. However, when she met Simon Dubin, she knew she had found someone who shared her beliefs. He believed passionately in the dignity and equality of all people; men and women, Jew and Gentile, black and white, rich or poor.

Though young Alick never had a mother waiting for him at the kitchen door, a plate of cookies in hand, there were compensations for being raised in the undomestic, intellectual atmosphere. Often, when visitors were in the parlor, Alick was not only allowed but

encouraged to delay his bedtime and visit with the adults, who were usually political activists, distinguished physicians, devotees and practitioners of the arts.

During one such evening, Alick was introduced to an intense, bearded man, who had come to the United States to attempt to raise support for the socialist cause. The man, Simon Dubin explained to his son, was named Alexy, but he used the name Maxim Gorky, and he was a very famous Russian playwright. Gorky had already written the famed *Lower Depths* but it had not yet been translated into English. Alick was rather more impressed that Mr. Gorky earned his daily bread with his writings than he was with the fact that Gorky was a potent political force.

Simon Dubin was becoming something of a celebrity, not only as a gynecologist, but as a political activist, organizing a group of Philadelphians who were in sympathy with the Revolution when Russian peasants attempted to break the yoke of Czarism. Often there were meetings at the family home on Pine Street. On one such occasion, Alick was awakened from sleep by shouts and crying from the parlor. He put on a robe and, barefoot, quietly descended the stairs and looked in the room where the meeting was being held. No one noticed the boy because they were so intent on what they were doing and saying. There were two people, a man and a woman, standing in the center of the room; the man had exposed the woman's back to show cruel scars that she had evidently received from numerous beatings. Alick gathered she had worked for a member of the landed gentry in Russia and her beatings were considered "all right" because she was a member of the "peasant" class.

The incident impressed the boy and he determined not to ever become a member of the "aristocracy" if the aristocracy perpetrated such cruelties. And yet, with a doctor-father and a chemist-mother, he knew he was not a peasant. Alick never resolved the dilemma, never emotionally realized that he did not have to rigidly choose between peasant and aristocrat; that aristocrats could be benign.

In later life he wore fine clothes; earned big money; owned a fancy car. But he insisted on eating ravenously, drinking loudly and spitting tobacco juice so he would not be mistaken for one of those aristocratic "bad guys" who felt superior to any member of the "lower classes."

"Look," Al was saying, "though I've got money, I'm really one of you. See, I spit and chew, and sometimes eat with my hands."

Another facet of life that confused Alick at this time was his parents' strong emphasis on the discipline of learning and science and the chaotic way in which the household was run. For instance:

"Alick," called his mother, Minna. "It is time for dinner."

"What are we having?" asked the boy.

"A nice, plump, juicy roast chicken," she tempted.

"I don't want chicken. I want a steak."

"Now, Alick, we have chicken."

"I told you," he said, petulantly now, "that I'm not in the mood for chicken. I ate chicken at my friend's house last night. I want a steak!"

This conversation would go on for a while with Simon finally intervening, asking his wife to see that the maid went to the store and got Alick his steak.

"After all," Simon would say, "what difference does it really make? Give the boy what he wants."

It was quite a shock to adolescent Al when he discovered the rest of the world did not play by his family's rules and, unfortunately, if not tragically, for Al Dubin, he kept trying all his life to manipulate circumstances in his favor and to gratify his smallest desire instantly. Simon and Minna had taught him his lessons too well.

On the other hand, Al would notice when he was at his friend's house that the mother would often serve them a snack or offer a plate of candy and act interested in their ballgame; ask questions. When he took a friend to his home, his mother was either not there or too busy or distracted to be the least bit interested that Al had just hit a grand-slam home run. The message was always the same: "Don't bother me; my work is important, but you are just a little boy who does not matter much."

On the one hand, his childish demands were granted; on the other, his human needs went unmet.

Though his parents were not religious Jews, they insisted that he be Bar Mitzvahed as a cultural rite of passage when he was thirteen years old.

It was entirely fitting, coming from such a household, that Alick developed a strong sense of justice, fair play and respect for the equality of all people. In his elementary school days, Alick was a bright student, doing particularly well in English and Spelling. He took great pride in winning spelling bees; he already was developing a love affair with words. The other top speller in the class was a black boy named Russell whom Al admired and respected. They competed often with Al winning one time, Russell another. At one match, the competition, as usual, narrowed down to Russell and Al.

The teacher gave Russell the word "R-O-E," but did not define it. Naturally, Russell spelled it "R-O-W."

"Wrong!" said the teacher, "Al?" And, of course, Al spelled "R-O-E," as it was the only possible answer. Russell said nothing, but walked to the coat closet in back of the classroom, took his jacket and cap and walked out. No one said a word and no one tried to stop him.

Alick knew the situation was wrong, but said nothing out of a Jewish boy's learned respect for all teachers. Years later, Alick saw Russell in downtown New York traffic, driving a truck.

"I wanted to cry over the waste of it," Al said. "Russell was the brightest student in the class, hands down, but because he was colored he didn't win that spelling bee. I've just never gotten over feeling guilty about the whole thing."

Along with his passionate love of sports—running, baseball and football games played after school on Philadelphia's streets—Alick developed an interest in reading. At the same time, he experienced a need to create something, feeling a stronger and stronger pull towards the artistic and less and less interest in the scientific. It could have been a quite natural rebellion against his scientific parents who expected him to conform to their way of life or it could have been a genetic disposition towards the verbal. It could have been a combination of the two.

At any rate, a growing need to communicate grew as the boy grew.

Simon's cousin, David, was fond of the young Alick and sensed his literary bent from the boy's dreamy reveries and his interest in the written word. Alick did not

read books, he devoured them. David noted this and presented Alick with a subscription to *St. Nicholas Magazine* for his birthday. To say Alick was pleased was an understatement. He read every line of each issue, and by the time the third one had arrived, he decided to enter one of the several contests the magazine offered its young readers. For his first entry, he drew a picture and it was rejected as prize material.

Though many youngsters would have given up at this rejection, the tenacity that was to characterize his later life as lyricist-in-residence for the brothers Warner asserted itself. This time he tried a cartoon. He thought it was very clever; the judges did not.

Still determined, Alick cajoled the Polish girl, Mary, to get him paints and paper. Though he had no sense of color or proportion, he was wildly enthusiastic about his painting of flowers as he spilled paint all over his good pants and the bedroom rug.

Mary chastised him gently. She loved Alick and had taught him the Catholic prayer, the "Hail Mary," which she recited with him each night. She also tried to calm his irrational but terrifying fear of the dark, a fear he never lost, by telling him he had a Guardian Angel that was with him always to protect him.

Simon and Minna did not approve of such "nonsense" but they were so busy with their own careers and causes that they did not interfere with Mary and her saints and Virgin.

Mary encouraged Alick to enter all the contests in the *St. Nicholas Magazine,* and though he prayed to both his Jewish God and his Catholic Guardian Angel, and spit for luck to boot, he still failed to win a prize.

Alick would not give up. However, the young boy was pretty philosophical about his inability to draw or paint, and decided this time he would write a short story. He wanted a prize. Though his story was much better than his painting and drawing, still there was no prize.

Now Alick was really getting discouraged. He was down to the last category in the *St. Nicholas Magazine*. That category was poetry.

Poetry! Alick thought that was for girls. But he read all the poems in the magazine and sat at the small table in his bedroom and wrote a poem about springtime. His verse, though trite in theme, boasted interesting and clever rhymes.

Alick received a bronze medal for his poem—the third place prize! It was the incentive he needed to continue to write poems. He enjoyed writing them and quickly discovered he had a knack for meter and rhyming. His parents smiled indulgently at this stage young Alick was going through. Like baseball, he would outgrow it or it would be a nice hobby for him, a form of relaxation after an exhausting day working in the hospital.

Eventually, Alick hit the jackpot. He won the gold medal, first prize, representing the best poem in the *St. Nicholas Magazine*. Al Dubin was hooked. He had fallen madly in love with rhyming, a love affair that lasted all his life. Although he did not know it, his life's work had begun.

Though Alick was very fond of his baby brother, his relationship with his mother did not improve after Joseph's birth. She seemed still colder, less accessible to him, busier with her work. But, shyly, he admired Si-

mon and began to take an interest, if not in "doctoring," at least in some of Simon's theories.

Al watched patients come to the house, ailing with common complaints of stomach pains and headaches. He watched Simon dispense small pink pills; then the patients would return, feeling much better, grateful to Dr. Dubin. Al asked his father if these were "magic" pills, but Simon laughed and confided to his son that they were sugar pills.

"These pills are nothing. No medicine in them. But the mind is very, very powerful, Alick. These people trust me. They think that I am giving something to make them well and so their minds heal their bodies. That is how it works. I do not have much medicine to cure sick people. My medicine is psychology—knowing they want to get well and knowing they believe in me. That way they get better."

Though Alick did not completely comprehend, he was impressed. He also was impressed with his father's ability to hypnotize his patients. Alick felt very important when his father allowed him in his office to watch a powerful demonstration of the hypnotic art.

A young woman, with beautiful long red hair, was seated in a massive leather chair. Dr. Dubin had hypnotized her. Her eyes were closed and young Alick watched, spellbound, as his father took an unlighted cigarette and told the woman that he was going to burn her bare arm. He touched her with the unlighted cigarette and she winced. Al's eyes widened with disbelief and awe, for when his father withdrew the cigarette, the woman had a burn mark. He became a believer in hypnosis though he was never able to incorporate it for good into his own life.

Alick's parents were brilliant people, constantly experimenting—Minna with diet and chemical formulas and Simon with hypnosis and psychology and nontraditional forms of medicine.

Minna experimented one time with an exclusive carrot diet and turned the color of one in the process of the experiment. This was in her later years, after I was born, and I remember being both impressed and horrified at the tiny yellow woman—four feet, eleven inches tall with a "natural" black hairstyle—sitting in a hospital bed, telling me what a brilliant baby my father had been. Minna outlived her firstborn son by many years and died in a California sanitarium in her late eighties.

Simon also experimented and examined and explored what medical evidence was available to him. He pointed out to Al—and this at the turn of the 20th century—that he should never smoke cigarettes because, though he felt the tobacco was not harmful, there was something in the paper that could cause lip, tongue and throat cancer. Though Al's adult life was characterized by excesses of every kind, he never smoked a cigarette.

The brilliance of his parents intimidated Alick. All that skill and talent left him feeling inadequate. Also angry. Inadequate in that he could not measure up to his immigrant parents' dreams for him as a skilled surgeon and angry that he was given so little emotional nourishment and support for his own feelings.

Rhyming took more and more of Alick's time and attention, and Simon was less and less impressed. Nonetheless, young Alick's passion for words continued

to take priority in his life, despite lack of parental approval. His was a courageous rebellion.

But Al was not the stereotype of the little boy who reads, wears thick glasses, has no friends, is clumsy and awkward in sports and games, abhors competition. He was a picture of the competitive athlete, good at games and sports, popular with his peers, as well as the reader-writer. He had a tremendous amount of energy that enabled him to pursue all of his interests.

Al loved to explore the city of Philadelphia. He visited Independence Hall and gazed with awe upon the cracked Liberty Bell. He walked the residential areas where solid row houses characterized the Philadelphia landscape. He and a friend put flowers on Benjamin Franklin's grave, wandered through the Betsy Ross house, William Penn's house. He would bring a lunch from home to eat in Logan Square or Rittenhouse Square or Fairmount Park. He was a curious boy, noticing everything in his environment, and he eventually noticed sheet music displayed in stores in the main section of the city. Often there was a piano player belting out the songs to induce customers to pay ten cents for a copy of the latest hit. He would often stand for an hour, listening, munching on a kosher dill pickle, cap pulled down to hide his protruding ears and as protection against Philadelphia's frosty winter.

He was hypnotized by the rhymes, the meter, the cadence. The germ of an idea was born. Could he write lyrics like that? He was pretty sure he could not compose the music. Though the Dubins did not own a piano, Al started buying the sheet music with his spare dimes and spending his time at the house of a friend,

Herman Goldberg, who did have a piano. Hermie and Al attended Hebrew School together and both were distracted, disinterested and bored by the experience. Hermie had very little time to spare as he also took piano and violin lessons. His immigrant parents dreamed of a future famous musician. So the two boys who were supposed to grow up to be, respectively, a surgeon and a musician, began to cut Hebrew School to hang out at Hermie's house. Hermie's parents were owners of a delicatessen and, because they worked long hours, the boys often had the house to themselves. Hermie taught Al, a poor but eager pupil, the rudiments of reading music. What he lacked in musical talent, Al made up in enthusiasm and was soon able to pick out tunes with one finger. When he could not read the little black notes, or if he wanted to hear the chords or left hand, Hermie would forsake Bach for popular music to satisfy his friend.

Al became obsessed with the songs, and would often write new lyrics to the tunes to see if he could improve on what was there. He had to serve as his own judge and jury, or ask Hermie's opinion of his lyrics. Hermie always had the same answer: "Very good."

Al was more critical and sometimes he felt he succeeded, while at other times he felt he had failed. He came to admire lyricists who were able to wed words to music so well that one could not imagine any other lyric fitting those notes. It looked easy, but he soon found out there was a trick to it. The trick was a combination of talent and hard work. Soon, along with the ERA (earned run average) of his favorite baseball pitchers, he knew the names of current popular lyricists and composers—names like Henry Blossom (who wrote lyr-

ics for the melodies composed by Victor Herbert), Will Cobb (author of "School Days"), George M. Cohan, Bob Cole, Paul Dresser, Charles Harris (author and composer of "After the Ball"), Robert B. Smith, William Jerome, Louis Hirsch and Theodore Morse.

He was growing fast, too fast for his short pants. When he was only twelve years old, he looked like a man of twenty, and bragged to his friends that if he could just get into long pants, he knew the Philadelphia saloon keepers would serve him. Al had already sampled liquor at that tender age and it was love at first taste. So, not quite thirteen years old, five feet, nine inches tall, weighing in at 175 pounds, the budding songwriter was allowed to don long pants.

Long pants became his entry into the adult world. Bartenders did indeed serve him and, as an added bonus, the ladies looked at him with interest.

Young Al loved the saloons, not only for the booze, but for the feeling of camaraderie that existed, the sense of acceptance he felt. He also enjoyed the free lunches. One dozen hard-boiled eggs at a sitting was standard for Al. Never a sweet-eater, he loved deli food, pastrami sandwiches on good Jewish rye, kosher dill pickles, pickled pigs' feet.

From the years thirteen to fifteen, Al ran the streets of Philadelphia, frequented the bars, played baseball and jogged through Fairmount Park, saw every sporting event that came to the city, ditched school frequently to see musical shows in New York City, and wrote special material for a Broadway vaudeville entertainer when he was only fourteen years old.

Al was busy serving his apprenticeship, as it were, on 28th Street between Fifth and Broadway in New York.

The area was nicknamed Tin Pan Alley. There, Al got acquainted with the various publishing firms, occasionally was lucky enough to talk to a singer in search of special material for a show or cabaret act. Because he looked so much older than his age, no one questioned his right to be there. For him, Tin Pan Alley soon became a natural habitat.

No geometry and algebra for him; not for him the stuffy schoolroom of rigid routine and discipline. Al was taking in the shows—*The Tattooed Man, Lola From Berlin, Hip! Hip! Hooray!, The Hoyden, Mam'selle Sally*. Al wondered how anyone could waste time working algebraic problems when all the glamor of the world of show business was just a train ride away from "Philly."

As Al moved turbulently through adolescence, he and his father clashed over the direction Al's life was taking. Simon was offended by his son's insistence on hanging about Tin Pan Alley instead of studying for his "proper" future profession of doctor. Al disliked the confrontations with Simon and did everything he could to avoid them. The more Simon pressed, the more determined Al became to pursue his career as a lyricist. He realized he was financially dependent on his father, that he could not support himself with lyrics yet, but had no doubt he would be able to do so in the future. So Al enrolled in Northeast M.T. High School, a trade or vocational school, reasoning that he would learn a trade to support himself while he was writing and peddling his lyrics.

Simon and Minna were horrified that they had a son in a trade school. They demanded, pleaded, threatened, bribed, negotiated. Al stood firm.

So, as he celebrated his sixteenth birthday in the summer of 1907, Al was rebellious, charming, enthusiastic about life and had many interests. He knew that he didn't want to miss a thing in life; he wanted to experience everything there was to experience—the thrills and excitement he found in getting high on alcohol; the lift to the spirit that poetry gave to him; the enchantment of plays, short stories; the vigorous pleasure of competitive sports like football, baseball, track; the soft and pretty girls with their long hair and teasing smiles. He wanted to do it all. He also knew he had to make it on his own personal street of dreams—Tin Pan Alley.

Al Dubin thought the world was his own personal oyster on the half-shell when he was sixteen. However, the path of life for the budding songwriter was to take some unexpected and unpleasant turns.

TWO

TRAGEDY was to visit the Dubin household. Minna's widowed sister, Pearl, had emigrated from Russia to Philadelphia to make her home with her sister's family until she could learn the language and find employment. Alick noticed there was more laughter in the house after the arrival of Aunt Pearl. Also, Simon started spending more time at home.

Pearl did not look like her sister, Minna. She was taller, fairer-skinned, more willowy in body. Her hair was straighter and softer than his mother's, Alick noted. The only thing Alick didn't like about his Aunt Pearl was her laugh. She giggled in a most offensive fashion, he thought, but he noted that his father didn't seem to mind at all. Pearl was a good cook and made cabbage soup and matzoh a couple of times a week.

After a few months, Alick noticed that Aunt Pearl wasn't cooking as much; she seemed sad where before she had seemed so joyful. Perhaps she was having a great deal of trouble learning English. Al tried to help

her and found her an apt pupil; he thought she was sad because she missed her native country.

One morning, Al wakened to utter confusion, shouting, a strange doctor in the house, the coroner. The coroner!

Later on, Dr. Dubin gave the following story to the police and the press. Pearl, plagued by insomnia, had gone to the medicine cabinet in the bathroom for a sleeping draught. Declining to turn on the light so she would not wake the family, she reached for the wrong bottle, which contained rat poison. It had been a tragic error. Never again would he keep any poison within reach in his medicine cabinet, vowed Simon.

Young Al was not completely happy with this story and assumed, rightly or wrongly, in his teenage fantasy, that it was no accident, that his aunt had taken her life because she was madly, hopelessly in love with Simon Dubin. He continued to speculate on the theory in adult life and never really changed his mind. At any rate, he was both devastated and furious that such a catastrophic event occurred in his home. He also began to suspect, with painful misgivings, that his father was not a monogamous man.

When school resumed in the fall of 1908, Al did not return to Northeast M.T. High School. He had completed one semester. This fact he managed to keep secret from Simon for a time, but eventually his father discovered that his son was not attending school at all.

Simon tried to reason with Al, adopting a stern attitude as Al fidgeted in his father's study. Al was polite, but determined; courteous, but distant.

Simon tried another approach. Late at night, when the doctor felt in the mood to raid the icebox, he would

awaken Al, invite him to partake of the midnight feast, and deal with him on a friendly, man-to-man basis, appealing to the emerging adult in his son. Al treasured the times spent alone with his father in the kitchen on Pine Street, sitting at the white kitchen table, piling brisket or poultry and cheese between thick slices of pumpernickel bread.

Simon talked to his son about food, about diet. ("As soon as my patients begin to eat white bread, they get stomach trouble; they gain too much weight; they get sick. Always eat dark bread, Alick.") He talked to his son about his more interesting patients; his theories of medicine, eugenics, sex, fatherhood, Russia, politics, socialism. He stopped alluding at all to the fact that his son was a school dropout.

He tentatively broached the subject of future employment. How was Al going to support himself and, eventually, a wife and, possibly, children?

Al would name some occupation sure to offend his father—like bartender. He never failed to get a rise out of Simon with this game.

They discussed professions from rabbi to wrestler—sometimes seriously, often in jest.

However, if Al came close to sharing his ambitions of writing songs, Simon dismissed them as trivial, out of the question. When Simon pressed too hard, Al withdrew.

Finally, Al convinced Simon that the confinement of school was unbearable. There was too little time for sports; he had had a dreadful English teacher who was not as well read as Al. Al assured Simon that he was educating himself, reading two or three books a week, writing essays, as well as poems—and lyrics.

He reminded his father of the poems that had been published in *St. Nicholas Magazine* as an indication that he could go on to bigger and better things in the future. He desperately wanted to convince this man that he could succeed in his chosen field.

So Simon stopped frowning temporarily, but he certainly wasn't smiling. He was filled with worried thoughts about Al and his future.

What Al didn't confide to Simon during their late night food feasts was the fact that he spent considerably more time taking the train to New York to go to vaudeville and burlesque shows than he did in Philadelphia's fine public libraries.

He was trying to sell special material to feature entertainers. (He had written a lyric used by a vaudevillian when he was only fourteen, but received no money for it.)

One night Al's efforts paid off. A female entertainer who was headlining at The Majestic paid Al five dollars for some special material. He was overjoyed. High on his success, he went every night to hear his material performed. The young boy felt a power he had never known. But still he managed to listen critically, and one night went backstage to suggest an improvement. The lady, half-way past thirty, thanked him for his interest. She invited the good-looking, shy, young boy to have a late supper with her in her apartment. Al was awed.

So after a supper that included a good deal of wine, Al showed the lady his skill as a lyricist and she responded by teaching him a thing or two about lovemaking. Al awoke in his songbird's Manhattan apartment thinking he now had two careers—lyrics and ladies.

Al didn't go home that day, but strolled into the nearest bar to celebrate both the loss of his virginity and the fact that he was truly a professional lyricist.

When he finally returned to Pine Street at four a.m., very drunk, Simon was waiting.

A scene ensued with the drunken Al hurling insults at his father, accusing him of adultery and lying, accusing him of taking an interest in his son's whereabouts much too late. Simon berated Al for his drunken and slovenly appearance. Minna appeared to try to make peace, urging Simon to try to understand the boy who had made a mistake that she was sure he would not repeat.

The next night, Simon tried to talk to Al. But Al wanted only to brag about the sale of special material to Lady X.

"But, Alick, a man doesn't give his life to rhymes and jingles. Maybe plays, poetry, novels—that is important work—but jingles, lyrics, no, no, that is not a man's work. You do not give your life to it." So spoke Simon Dubin to his son who had just confided to his father that he was now a professional lyricist.

"I want to write lyrics. I'm good at it," Al told Simon. "I don't want to be a doctor. I want to write songs."

"But, Alick," Simon said, taking his son's hands in his own, "look at those wonderful hands! They are the hands of a surgeon. So few men have surgeon's hands. You were born to be a doctor, Alick. Forget this lyric nonsense."

Nonsense! His dreams were "nonsense" to his father.

Bringing pleasure or joy to others was not Dr. Dubin's idea of a well-spent life. Though Al disagreed violently, his father's voice haunted him all his life, and at the very

pinnacle of his Hollywood success, he denigrated what he did so well, saying about songwriting, "If it is art, it is the very lowest form of art."

Teenage tenacity and exuberance, coupled with lyrical talent, paid off for Al and in 1909 Witmark published his first two songs, "Prairie Rose" and "Sunray."

If he thought he had proved something to Simon, he was wrong. Simon continued to plead with Al to get himself back to school, offering to pay for a private school if Al could find one that suited him.

Al selected Perkiomen Seminary, a private preparatory school located in Pennsburg, forty miles north of Philadelphia. It was a strange choice for a Jewish boy, albeit one who absorbed only the culture, not the religion.

The school, founded in 1875 by Reverend C.S. Wieand of Pottstown, Pennsylvania, was purchased by the Schwenkfelder Church in 1891 and opened its doors to young men and women as a resident and day school in 1892.

On August 11, 1909, Al Dubin wrote the following letter to Perkiomen.

Rev. Kriebel,
Have completed one year at the Northeast M.T. High School of Philadelphia. Have been away from school two years and would now like to enter a private preparatory school to complete my course.
Would you kindly send me all necessary information and data immediately, for in case I should decide to enter your school, I would like to do so without delay.
Do you accept Hebrews as students? I am a Hebrew by birth although not brought up in the Jewish faith.

I'm eighteen years of age. Awaiting an early reply I remain,

> Respectfully,
>
> Alexander Dubin
> 325 Pine Street
> Philadelphia, Pa.

Young Alexander Dubin was accepted at Perkiomen in September of 1909. New suitcase in hand, packed by the Dubin's housekeeper, Al stepped off the train on a lovely eastern fall day to begin an academic life.

Prepared to hate the place, he soon fell in love with Perkiomen—with the young ladies, the athletic program, the extracurricular activities. He even attended classes (and enjoyed some of them) when the spirit moved him.

His need to excel found all kinds of positive outlets at the school. Here he could call on his varied talents, experience different parts of himself, forget some of the pain of the past. However, his exuberance jumped the line into undisciplined behavior and Perkiomen wasn't any more ready for the budding lyricist than Warner Brothers was to be many years later. Al Dubin did things well, to be sure, but he did them his way. If his way happened to be your way, there was no problem. However, his way it had to be, and I don't think even he knew why this had to be so.

In two years Al Dubin became a name to be reckoned with. He was captain of the football team, playing fullback; captain of the track team, placing first in the 100-yard dash, as well as the 440-yard relay. He played both forward and center positions on the basketball

team and received letters for all the above sports, missing out only on baseball and tennis.

He was an associate editor of both the school newspaper *The Perkiomenite* and the yearbook *The Griffin,* contributing verses, stories, and songs to both.

He won a prize for short story writing, composed both the class poem and the class song, wrote the Alma Mater, which is still sung by current Perkiomen students, constantly "stole social privileges" with the young ladies, got drunk with the boys and was expelled a few days before graduation.

His class yearbook notes that he was famous for cutting classes; his hobby was getting into trouble and, prophetically: "Al is a star—nay he is a whole constellation unto himself. But oh! Al, in no way dost thou more resemble a star than in thy proneness to fall!"

Al's roommate at the school was a thirteen-year-old boy named Clarence Hillegasse, whose parents were separated and whose mother lived in Allentown, Pennsylvania. On weekends, eighteen-year-old Al would go to Allentown with young Clarence, feeling more comfortable there than he did in Philadelphia with a mother who ignored him and a father who disapproved of what he wanted to do with his life. Al behaved himself when he was with young Clarence, obeying all the rules and enjoying his weekends with "the kid." The fact that Clarence's folks were separated helped Al to relate. Sometimes he felt that he lived in a world peopled with loving, caring, supportive, concerned parents and he was the only one who had a "different" background.

Though Simon was not supportive of Al's desire to be a lyricist, he was nonetheless greatly concerned about his son's progress in school and wrote to Reverend O.S. Kriebel, the principal, for a progress report. Kriebel replied in October, 1909: "His work in Latin is very good. He is improving very much in his German and his work in rhetoric is first-class. He is doing good work in chemistry. I understand that your son has considerable literary ability and, because of that, he was selected as assistant editor on our school paper, *The Perkiomenite.*"

By March of 1910, the exuberant Al was in trouble at Perkiomen. It seems four boys and four girls slipped out and "stole social privileges." Because of the hanky-panky, Al was to be sent home, forbidden to take his examinations. He was to return in the spring, take special examinations and pay extra for the privilege.

Al told Reverend Kriebel that he was afraid to go home, that he couldn't face his father. So Kriebel wrote to Dr. Dubin saying, "I simply want to say a good word on his behalf. I want you to know that we have confidence in the boy and believe that he ought to be encouraged to continue."

This is precisely the kind of letter Al wanted his father to receive and knew that by telling Kriebel he was "afraid" to face his father he could manipulate events in his favor. To gain his father's sympathy, he would tell him how he feared Kriebel, thus getting both men on his side.

Dr. Dubin, as Al expected, was gracious about the punishment and was really more concerned with Al's chemistry grades; he still harbored expectations that his son would follow in his footsteps and become a doctor.

While Al was experiencing difficulties with those in authority, he was building a network of friends and admirers among his classmates. Ruth Kaufman, a day student, developed a tremendous crush on the handsome, athletic Al, and followed him around the campus with dogged devotion. But Al, who magnanimously played the field, in turn developed a crush on Helen Reich, who was already "promised" to someone else.

After her marriage, Helen moved to Bakersfield, California, and Al and Helen saw each other several times after their Perkiomen days. He always held a soft spot in his heart for the beautiful young lady.

All the students were fond of Al. His classmates who are still living describe him as a "very happy-go-lucky kind of person."

"He was such a colorful character," "He walked with such a special stride," were some of the comments. In the language of "now," I suppose one could say the young man had charisma.

Al published verses in almost every issue of the school paper and the following is representative of the kind of verse he was turning out as a teenager.

THE DREAMER

The dreamer oft is pitied

We sometimes wonder why—
For dreaming is a pathway
To roam—for you and I.
Oh, dreaming dreams is pleasant,
But just remember, too—
Dream those dreams while dreaming,
Then make them all come true.

For dreaming cannot bring us
The things of which we dream—
But dreaming can awaken us
To action, it would seem.
If we craved the goal of Fancy
As dreamers always do—
Dream those dreams while dreaming—
Then make them all come true!

After Al had discovered the works of Alfred, Lord Tennyson, in an English literature class, specifically the *In Memoriam* that contains the famous lines:

Tears, idle Tears,
I know not why they fall.

he was inspired to respond:

TEARS

Tears, Tears—are not idle tears,
Yet so it has been said—
Eyes are human safety valves
And tears were made to shed.

Hearts would break with grief and pain,
But tears relieve the heart—
And take the sadness with them,
By Nature's subtle art.

A little quiet weeping
If done once in a while
Takes a burden off your soul—
Leaves in its place a smile.

Or this highly sentimental, stylized verse.

DO YOU REMEMBER, PAL OF MINE

Just picture a woodland,
A rock and a stream—

With high bending poplars,
The moon's gentle beam.
Remember the voices
We heard from afar—
The crystalline twinkle
Of each little star.

Just picture yourself, pal,
As I picture you—
A sweet tender vision,
Eyes of perfect blue.
Recollect what we talked of
In that lonely dell—
When we told the secrets
Pals alone can tell.

I know I remember,
Never can forget.
But oft as I ponder
There is one regret—
Maybe you've forgotten,
While I long and pine—
Or do you remember,
Dear old pal of mine.

The following is an excerpt from a verse entitled "The Mate of His Soul."

She was the mate my soul had craved
Her heart was akin to mine,
She saw the world with my very eyes
Yet I missed her all the time.

I woke at last from an empty dream
But there was no vain regret,
For though I knew it was Fancy—all,
There's the hope I'll meet her yet.

Or this excerpt from "We Have Power to Forget."

"Worry" is a spider sly,
Each of us a little fly—
So beware now of his net—
We have power to forget.

Al was pretty much in command of things at Perkiomen, and the only thing he didn't seem able to handle, besides keeping the rules, was Algebra and Geometry. He hated both subjects. So because Al was doing poorly, Reverend Kriebel suggested he attend summer school:

> I notice that your son is back in Mathematics, especially in Algebra, also in Geometry and it is of the utmost importance that he take up work in Algebra and Geometry this summer if he is to complete his work satisfactorily for graduation next year. In fact, the boy left school just before Commencement time, with the distinct understanding, I believe, that he would be back for summer school. I am anxious to know, therefore, why he did not report last week, also when we may expect him. It will be a very great mistake, in my judgment, if your son would not take up work in Algebra and Geometry this summer.

Al and Simon had discussed the summer school issue and Al fully intended to attend. But he met a friend who asked him to come to Arden, Delaware, where a colony of writers, artists and philosophers had gathered to lecture and discuss the arts and problems of living— all in a forest setting. Al wrote:

> I am away from all city influences among intellectual people and in daily contact with such men as Upton Sinclair, Professor Scott Nearing, Professor of Economics at the University of Pennsylvania; George Brown, the Shoemaker philosopher; Howe, "the millionaire

hobo" whom I heard speak last night. Each night, lectures, followed by discussions, are held in a woodland by the light of the heavens where most cultured men and women sit upon the ground in comfortable garb, such as overalls and bloomers, discussing vital questions of life.

I, together with a friend of mine, am living close to nature, cooking all our meals and existing on healthy, wholesome food. We put up our canvas home ourselves and now I hate to leave it. I am now also rehearsing a part in *Romeo and Juliet* which I must play in the cast together with the rest of the young people of Arden. Other plays are anticipated in the near future to be produced in the woodland theatre.

So you can readily see that the project of geometry does not contrast favorably with my present situation and I would not leave it for the world. I will return to school in September.

Wishing you and the school success, I remain,

Loyal to Perkiomen,

AL DUBIN

Al was fascinated with a young adult's fascination by Upton Sinclair and was delighted when Sinclair befriended him. Al was pleased to learn that he was a sports-minded man who enjoyed a game of baseball now and again. In fact, Upton Sinclair and Al Dubin, along with several others, were arrested in Philadelphia one Sunday for playing baseball and spent some time locked up in the local jail together.

If the summer was a nineteen-year-old's dream of the good life, the fall was not to prove so auspicious. Al's unreliability grew. He started leaving school without permission, even missing football games and practices.

In October of 1910, Kriebel wrote the following to Dr. Dubin:

The boy has been very careless about matters on the whole, frequently neglecting to do things that he is told to do and I have just told him that if he could not meet his appointments and do his work promptly and regularly that is assigned to him, and obey the rules and regulations of the school that he would be sent home without any further ceremony. We certainly must not let him go on in this slip-shod way. One of the first things the boy has to learn is obedience and learn to obey the rules and regulations. He is capable of doing excellent work and it is a pity that he does not hold himself down more firmly.

An annoyed and grieving Simon answered Dr. Kriebel immediately: "I am very grieved to hear that Alick gives you cause for annoyance. He made me believe that he is fulfilling everything that is required of him."

While Al continued to collide with voices of authority, his popularity and proficiency in many different areas continued to expand.

In his middle years, Al made fun of his off-key singing voice, just as he did of his excess weight. But at Perkiomen he was a member in good standing of the Glee Club and received "thunderous applause" for his singing of "Cease, Sweetheart, Cease" in a minstrel show produced by the Glee Club on December 16, 1910.

The day before the Glee Club performance, Al had distinguished himself in a basketball game against Southern High which Perkiomen won 46 to 16, by

shooting three field goals and putting away four foul-line baskets.

He continued as captain of the football team, scoring touchdowns by carrying the ball through the line against such schools as Northeast Manual and Farm School.

In this excerpt from *The Perkiomenite*, Al's ability is noted.

Capt. Dubin, alias "Al, the songwriter," etc., etc., was one of our few veterans this season. His aptness and agility made him a valuable factor as a speedy back for the receiving of forward passes; he also showed much ability as a line plunger. Al seemed at all times to be in the game and, indeed, improved in ability from week to week. Possibly the best form shown by him was in the Pennington game, when he repeatedly carried the ball for long gains and at all times gave remarkable interference. In the Swarthmore game, he proved himself a powerful defensive player.

Al took on still another activity at Perkiomen as athletics editor for *The Perkiomenite*. After a trip to Philadelphia to compete in a basketball game with the University of Pennsylvania, Al would go back to Pennsburg to write up notes on the game, always hoping for a glimpse of the beautiful, fun-loving Helen Reich, who had become an associate editor of *The Perkiomenite*.

Though Al took on more and more activities with seemingly inexhaustible energy, an aura of irresponsibility still lurked about him. When he travelled with the team for basketball games, he performed well, wanted

his team to win, was one of the guys. But he usually had a bottle of liquor with him. Sometimes when he went off to sing with the Glee Club to Quakertown or Harleysville or Tamaqua, he would slip away to get drunk. On one occasion he even managed to lose his rented dress suit; he claimed he had no recollection of where he left it. Simon, protesting, was charged for the suit.

When Al managed to make a Glee Club performance, he not only sang, but composed special lyrics. One night, with an engagement in Norristown on the agenda, Al was a no-show and his friends composed the following lyrics to cover for him:

"We sang some local hits last year [Al's songs], and now I guess you'll shake with fear; don't be afraid for it's all right, the fellow who writes them is sick tonight."

The first short story Al wrote, "Wonder Girl" was published in *The Perkiomenite*. It was well written, suspenseful, but he never tried to write another. Short stories were not as much fun for him as lyrics, not as challenging. Also, though he could accept the discipline of putting a lyric to music, working within the confinement of thirty-two bars, he did not enjoy the discipline of plotting a short story.

In fact, Al did not enjoy discipline of any kind that was imposed on him by the external world. He was frustrating his teachers; he was clearly a challenge to Reverend Kriebel, who simply could not understand Al Dubin's wild ways.

In December of 1910, Kriebel wrote the following letter to Dr. Dubin:

He really has a remarkable ability along a great many
different lines, chiefly, however, along literary lines. He
has originality and resourcefulness. If the boy would
spend half as much time on his studies as most students
are obliged to do, he could probably make perfect
marks in almost every subject that he has, and still have
plenty of time for outside work—for general reading
and diversions. If he could only be made to see the necessity of doing those things, if he could only be induced
to pursue such a course of strict discipline with himself,
it would be the best possible thing that could happen.

The holiday season of that year was a good one in the
Dubin household. Simon and Minna were proud of
their firstborn son and Simon generously gave Al
money to enjoy himself ushering in the New Year.
Though he was hung over on the first day of 1911, Al
thought it would be a great year for him.

As spring erupted in Pennsylvania, teenaged Al was
in his adolescent glory at Perkiomen. In spite of repeated warnings from Kriebel and his professors, he
continued to do what he wanted to do, when he wanted
to do it.

As Al awoke one beautiful March Sunday morning to
the smell of spring, his favorite time of year, he asked
for permission to go uptown to church. He had no in-
tention of attending church services, but he knew permission would be granted for such a spiritual request.
Spirituality was not what Al had in mind, however. He
knew of a local park where pretty girls walked in their
long dresses on a Sunday afternoon. Introducing himself with all the charm he was capable of, Al had no
trouble convincing a couple of girls to join him for "just
a glass or two of beer." One or two beers led to one or

two more, followed by a late supper. Then one of the girls knew of an unoccupied apartment that belonged to a friend of a friend. Consequently, Al didn't stumble into his room at Perkiomen until well past midnight after his glorious day of wine, women and spring songs.

Kriebel was furious enough to suspend him:

My dear Mr. Dubin:

I suppose by this time you know your son has been suspended from school for the rest of the term . . . . Unless the boy is willing to do some good, hard studying at the beginning of next term, and unless the boy gives me positive assurance that he will attend strictly to business in the matter of cutting classes and neglecting his work, I shall not let him continue at all. It is not right for us to allow any student to be a law unto himself with reference to classes, studies, habits, etc. We have all taken a deep interest in your son, and I think I have spent more hours in talking to him about his work than any other boy at the school.

Young Al and Simon Dubin clashed over the suspension incident and Al packed a bag and left home, going to the New Bingham Hotel at 11th and Market Streets in Philadelphia.

He took matters into his own hands and wrote Kriebel a masterful letter proclaiming great remorse over his actions, claimed he saw things in "a new light," and promised to observe all the rules if only he could return.

My dear Dr. Kriebel:

Acting on your request to repeat my avowal of yesterday I beg to say that I am exceedingly sorry for my actions of Sunday night as well as sorry for several previous actions.

Thinking the matter over I see things in a new light and have started work in preparation for my examina-

tions. I realize what it means to me to be dropped now and also realize what good the school has done for me.

If allowed to return I am perfectly willing to take every penalty imposed and will expect to be deprived of every school activity, barring none, as a punishment.

I am very thankful to you for past favors and hoping this will receive favorable consideration, I remain

> Sincerely,
>
> Al Dubin
> General Delivery
> Phila., PA

Kriebel was impressed and told Al to continue to study and he would re-admit him if he was willing to follow the rules. Al happily accepted.

He was back—back to his writing, his studies, his girl friends, and especially track, pehaps the most important activity in his life at that time.

On June 3rd, 1911, Al experienced a day of glory. He placed first in 100 yards and 220 yards and tied for first place in individual honors. Perkiomen had beaten St. Joseph's College of Philadelphia in the track meet and Al was very proud that he had contributed so much to that victory.

A huge bonfire was lighted on campus and each athlete walked to a platform to give a brief speech.

Al, his heart full, stood on the platform and thanked Perkiomen, his coaches, Dr. Kriebel, his teammates— for the opportunity to receive such honors:

"I know I sometimes cause others a lot of trouble, but I don't mean to, and I really love Perkiomen and all that the school stands for."

Al received a round of hearty applause, but he soon slipped away from his friends to go uptown to his favorite bar where he proceeded to get very drunk. The glory of the moment was not enough; he needed the high of liquor, both to celebrate victory and to comfort him in defeat or disappointment. Whiskey was playing an ever-increasingly important role in his life.

When eight o'clock curfew came, there was no Al. It was all an exasperated Kriebel needed. He expelled Al on June 4, 1911, just a few weeks before graduation, and a week before Al's twentieth birthday.

Kriebel, calling for a general assembly, formally and publicly expelled Al in front of his classmates, most of whom thought it was unfair—especially the girls— especially Ruth and Helen.

Al, bitter at the dismissal, denied some of the charges leveled against him while Kriebel stated in a letter to Simon: "As far as his work at Perkiomen Seminary is concerned, he forfeited his last opportunity and shut every door by his own foolish acts against himself."

Al found it hard to cope with the fact that he had been a hero one day, bringing honor and glory to the school with his outstanding athletic ability, and in disgrace the next.

Simon was angry. Al was sensitive. Off Al went to seek employment. But he was twenty years old. He missed the glory of winning the 100-yard dash, of writing love poems to the pretty girls, of being captain of the football team. Now that it was gone beyond his grasp, he wanted it all back. There was only one problem. Al Dubin wouldn't, or perhaps couldn't, pay the price others asked.

In any case, Al became obsessed with the idea of getting back into Perkiomen and wrote Rev. Kriebel a letter in September of 1911, pleading for another chance and stating he would pay his own tuition.

Dear Doctor:

I suppose you will be surprised to hear from me but nevertheless it is so.

First let me congratulate you on your initiation of your agricultural project, and also your large enrolment [sic]. It gratifies me greatly, although you may not believe it.

I will state my business bluntly, shortly and concisely.

I am now dependent on myself and not faring so very well. I know I am not deserving of much sympathy or consideration but remember there are such things as environment, inherent tendencies, etc. that make people what they are. A year of reverses has somewhat calloused me and taken away that super-exuberance that caused me so much trouble—so here is my proposition. You know that I am aware of the bill that still stands between you and my father. That is not however the point I wish to discuss.

I am anxious exceedingly anxious to undergo another year of your wise discipline (how well I see it now) and a year of good physical training under Prof. Daby, mainly. I do not mention studies for that comes under the head of discipline. I do not intend to go to college, as I have a business proposition in view which I cannot go into until I am twenty-one, which will be in June, 1912. This will not require any capital on my part and I will accept it. Until then a year of Perkiomen would do me a wealth of good.

Now, if I could enter immediately, I will pay you $20.00 (twenty dollars) down in advance, twenty-five dollars being my entire capital. I will work doing anything to work off the rest for the rest of the term. I will

pay $20.00 in advance of each term and work, mean-
while from time to time, working off the old debt of last
year by small payments which I am likely to receive
from the sale of songs.

I will do my utmost in helping the school in athletics,
literary work and as far as deportment and studies go—
give me a chance. I know it sounds like a mockery to
hear "Give Al Dubin a chance" but you have nothing to
lose and all to gain by the experiment. Impatiently
awaiting a reply, I remain

> Sincerely loyal to Perkiomen
>
> Al Dubin
> c/o Colonial Theatre
> Phila., PA

The line in the letter—"there are such things as environment, inherent tendencies, etc., that make people
what they are"—is more than a young man's immature
refusal to take responsibility for himself. Al, with all his
sardonic good humor, his tribute to joy in both songs
and life, never shook that feeling of impending doom,
that feeling that he would end up badly. It was almost as
if he were rehearsing a tragic script that had to be
played out to the end. If, during his lifetime, he enjoyed
his success, he never felt he deserved it.

Kriebel was impressed, as Al had figured he would
be; so impressed that he wrote Simon and asked him to
please reconsider and pay his son's tuition of the previous year to relieve Al of the burden. Though understanding, Kriebel was also a shrewd and practical man
and wrote Al, asking:

"What assurance do you have that you will be able to
pay? I understand you can find a ready sale for your

songs. What are your plans with reference to writing more songs? Will it be possible for you to earn considerable money in that way during the course of the year?"

These were overwhelming questions for a frightened, disillusioned twenty-year-old who had cut the ties with home.

Al went back to Perkiomen, but found promises made on paper were hard to keep. Discipline, no matter how much he talked about it, didn't come easily. He liked to go to town and drink; he liked to sleep late; liked to flirt with the girls; he liked to chew tobacco. He hated the routine of disciplined study, of working on algebraic equations, of daily chapel. But he was subdued and he was trying.

Meanwhile, Simon and Minna had moved to 1112 North 40th Street and Reverend Kriebel continued to write to him there until he agreed to pay his son's former debts.

In a letter of November 13, 1911, he said: "I am glad to be able to report that your son is doing much better . . . . I earnestly hope that he will not disappoint us, both on his own account, as well as on our account and on your account."

On November 20, 1911, Kriebel wrote the following letter to Al:

I notice your marks went down last week instead of up. Now, it is very evident we cannot go on at this rate. If it is impossible for you to do better work and make a more satisfactory showing, I shall be obliged to cancel my offer to you, because my offer was made with the distinct understanding on my part, and with the distinct promise on your part, that you would do satisfactory work in your studies, and that you would 'make good' in every

respect. You are not making good now, and I shall have
to write home to your father to the same effect. I shall
give you time until Thanksgiving to straighten the matter out. I am very sorry indeed, more so than I can say,
that you are not making good, because it looks to me
now that you will disappoint us in your last chance here
at Perkiomen Seminary. I have talked to you about this
matter, have urged it upon you, and have appealed to
you until I cannot do anymore.

O.S. Kriebel

Al spent the Thanksgiving Holidays with his family
and returned to school, determined to "make good."
But he just couldn't seem to do what was expected of
him.

Al was not only in debt concerning his tuition, but was
constantly borrowing small sums of money from the office clerks, from his roommate, from his football
friends. He was always broke, needing drinking money,
gambling money, date money. Perhaps he meant to pay
it back; Al just never got around to it.

The Perkiomen episode finally ground to a halt in
December of 1911. In despair, Reverend Kriebel wrote
to Simon: "I do not understand the boy. I thought he
was very serious about this matter but either he is not
able to control himself or else he does not care enough
about it to make a strong effort, or both."

It seemed that the riddle of Al Dubin's self-
destructiveness in the face of so much talent would
never be solved.

HIS SCHOLASTIC CAREER finished forever, Al knew he had to take on the world. It never occurred to him he would have to take it on on the world's terms; it would be, as always, on Al Dubin's terms. If such an attitude was unrealistic, he was in touch enough with reality to know he would have to make one big concession—he would have to support himself. He realized his father would not pay his rent or buy his groceries while he struggled to sell his words. Getting published in *The Perkiomenite* was one thing; selling a song to a publisher was quite another. So, capitalizing on his experience with the choral group at school, Al got himself a job as a singing waiter at a Philadelphia restaurant while he continued writing lyrics and trying to sell them to Welch & Wilsky, a Philadelphia publishing firm.

A milestone was marked in the professional life of Al Dubin the year he left Perkiomen. He met one Joseph Francis Burke, a talented but struggling composer, and

they collaborated on "Oh, You, Mister Moon" in 1911, which was published by M. Witmark & Sons. Joe Burke and Al became close friends and Joe, who was married and the father of a couple of small children, asked Al to come and live with them. Al was well liked in the household and soon became "that funny Uncle Sandy" to the Burke children.

Though Joe and Al wrote prodigiously, it was to be five years before they published another song together—"You're Like a Beautiful Song," with collaborator J.E. Dempsey on the lyrics. The following year, 1917, Joe and Al wrote "My Yiddish Butterfly," but to demonstrate his versatility ethnically, as well as lyrically, Al wrote that same year "My Irish Song of Songs" with Daniel Sullivan, and "Come Down to Tony Spagoni's Cabaret" with Clarence Gaskill.

Joe and Al, for recreation, often went for a swim in the cold Atlantic. Al proudly recounted the story of how Joe suffered a cramp one afternoon when he had gone very far from shore and Al rescued him. He told the story dramatically on several occasions. However, a member of the Burke family says, the basic story was true; it just wasn't Al who rescued Joe.

There are numerous apocryphal stories in the life of Al Dubin; he would change stories for effect, depending on the audience. One never knew if they were true or false. His friends either believed the stories or overlooked the fact that they were not true. The lies hurt no one.

Eventually, Al left the Burke residence to rent quarters of his own. Between his job as singing waiter, the sale of a song here and there, "loans" (seldom repaid) from friends, and an occasional assist from his father,

Al was managing to survive; not in luxury, to be sure, but he was making it after a fashion. He took his meals at the restaurant or at friends' homes; he lived in an inexpensive furnished room that he maintained in chaos. Books and magazines were strewn about the floor; dust covered everything, and cobwebs dangled from the ceiling. Soiled linen graced the permanently unmade bed. Dirty laundry and clean clothes were accorded the same careless attention—they were heaped indiscriminately together on the bed, the floor or stuffed into the closet. Empty whiskey bottles were everywhere, and tobacco juice stained the fading and peeling wallpaper. Personal grooming or housekeeping were items not ranked high on Al's priority list. A friend of his, dismayed at the messy surroundings, asked Al how he could live like that. Al responded that life was too short to spend it on non-essentials.

"You do what you can do best. For me, that's lyrics. And the rest of the time you enjoy yourself, have a good time. One hundred years from today, who the hell will care if you made your bed or washed out your socks?"

When life on the home front got totally out of control, Al would hire someone to clean up his mess. Later on in life when he enjoyed financial success, Al simply threw away soiled shirts and underwear when he was travelling, rather than go through the bother of sending them to a laundry. Life was too short for laundry lists.

Al's friends saw him during this period as a hard-drinking, tobacco-chewing, gluttonous, gambling man who had a passion for spectator sports, attending everything from boxing matches to the seven-day bike races.

At this time in Al's life, Joe Burke and a performer by the name of Benny Davis figured prominently. The

three men would toss ideas around for hours, trying to come up with that wonderful combination of simple melody, simple but provocative lyric; in short, a hit song. What did the public want? What would sell? What would a publisher take a chance on? Al soon had the title from Joe and Benny as "the idea man." His ideas didn't always work, but his imagination was fertile enough to turn them out by the dozen, seemingly effortlessly.

Soon it became clear to Al and Joe that, though the major song publishing firms maintained outlets in Philadelphia, the action was really in New York. This presented no problem to the footloose and fancy free Dubin, but for family man Burke it did. Nonetheless, Joe figured he had to support his family and he thought he could do it better by moving to New York. So Al packed up his dirty clothes, left the empty whiskey bottles and he and Burke moved to the Beacon Hotel in New York City where they tossed ideas around for five days a week and collaborated when one of those ideas proved fruitful. They moved a rented piano into the Beacon Hotel, though Burke often composed by whistling.

Joe Burke returned home to wife and kids on the weekends while Al concentrated on drinking, entertaining young ladies and having a good time. Not that he didn't drink and woo women during the week—he just exerted a more concentrated effort during weekends. But even when he was playing, Al's brain was working, working on a possible future lyric. Every experience was grist for the mill of his craft.

Shortly after he met Joe Burke, Al formed an association with publishers Jack and Irving Mills. He never

signed a contract with them but he came up with a creative idea that added revenue to the Mills's firm. Having
many "standard" compositions in their catalogue without
lyrics, the Millses listened to Al's suggestion that he put
lyrics to these classics and sell them for ten cents a copy, a
respectable price tag in the days prior to World War I. Al
always thought a song had more appeal, classics included, if there were lyrics to sing. He used to tell composer Harry Warren that "boy got girl" with the words he
whispered in her ear—not by humming the tune!

At any rate, Al penned lyrics to such classics as
"Cielito Lindo," "O Sole Mio," "La Golondrina," "A
Song of India." The Millses called it the Supreme Edi-
tion Catalogue and marketed it at Sears Roebuck,
Woolworth, Montgomery Ward and similar outlets.
The venture was successful.

Jack and Irving Mills brought the rights to a German
show that had grossed well at the box office and hired
Al Dubin to translate the lyrics and provide some special
material.

"Al was terrific with special material," said Irving
Mills. "He enjoyed turning out a clever extra verse or
chorus, and one of his best jobs was one he did for
Sophie Tucker in San Francisco. Sophie was an Orange
Queen and made her dramatic entrance in a spectacular
white fur coat. His special material for that was great,
very clever. Al always seemed to know what people
wanted. He had the real thing, talent. And I think he
was more prolific than almost any other lyricist back in
the old Tin Pan Alley days. He could really grind out
those lyrics."

One of the lyrics Al translated was called "It's Young
and It Doesn't Know." There was a scene in the show

built around a policeman, a nursemaid and a baby. The nursemaid is annoyed when the baby starts crying and fussing and the policeman sings her the song, asking her to be tolerant of the baby.

"I never forgot Al's lyrics, and I can recite them by heart to this day. I used to sing the song to my own children at night," reminisced Mills.

If a young Irving Mills was impressed with Al's talent, he was equally impressed in a negative way with Al's drinking bouts. One night Dubin landed at Dad's Hotel in Philadelphia, an establishment frequented by burlesque entertainers. He arrived there with a statuesque burlesque beauty, very drunk, and continued drinking, rampaging through the lobby until the manager threatened to throw him out. Al asked the manager to call Irving Mills in New York, who obligingly caught the next train for Philadelphia and brought Al back to New York. Al didn't care to discuss the episode.

It was to be the first of many such episodes with a repetitious pattern. Al would drink in a marathon-like contest with himself, stop eating, find his way to some hotel or hospital, stir up trouble with his erratic behavior and finally, threatened with expulsion, he would demand that someone call a friend, a publisher, a wife, a collaborator, a daughter—to bail him out.

The summer of 1916, one of Al Dubin's favorite lyrics was published. The title was " 'Twas Only an Irishman's Dream" and it was twenty-five-year-old Al's first modest hit. While celebrating the success of his song, Al was enjoying a free lunch in his favorite saloon in Philadelphia when a friend came in and showed him the *Philadelphia Inquirer* with a story slugged PROMINENT LOCAL PHYSI-

CIAN TO DIVORCE WIFE. The physician was his father. Al paled at the scandal of it. Men, in those days, did not divorce their wives. Al left his lunch unfinished, his beer glass half full, and hurried to see Simon.

Simon had fallen in love with a lady named Esther, the wife of an invalid patient of his. The man had long been in a wheelchair and the wife had cared for him solicitously, Simon explained, but he and Esther had fallen in love. Did Al really find that so difficult to understand? Yes, Al did. Fooling around with an invalid's wife in the invalid's home was not playing by the rules.

"And when did you ever play by the rules?" Simon asked his son.

"Maybe not playing by the rules is hereditary," screamed Al, slamming out of his father's house.

Simon's divorce became final in April of 1917, and he and Esther travelled to New York for the marriage ceremony to avoid any further talk or scandal in Philadelphia. Al did not attend the wedding. Simon and Esther Dubin settled down in a three-story house on Girard with Al's brother, Joseph.

Al, oddly, never mentioned Esther to anyone, and treated the incident of his father's remarriage as if it had never happened; and Esther, though she inherited all of Simon's estate, remains a woman shrouded in mystery.

At any rate, Al was not the only one to be shocked by Simon's divorce and subsequent hasty remarriage. Dr. Dubin lost many patients who sought a less flamboyant doctor to minister to their physical ills. Simon was emotionally shattered by the loss of trust in him by his son and by his patients.

Al, in his turn, used the divorce issue as an excuse for his own destructive way of life and also tripled his efforts to prove to Simon, now too defeated to respond, that lyrics could earn a man his daily bread.

Al published some thirty-two songs from the time he left Perkiomen to the time of his parents' divorce and, though some of them had sold well, none of them were "million copy" hits. Publication of "All the World Will Be Jealous of Me" in 1917 changed all that. Al had made his mark on Tin Pan Alley; he had arrived as a legitimate songwriting talent. Music for the song was composed by Ernie Ball, whom Al had long admired.

"Dream of a Soldier Boy," written with good friend James Monaco, and "Your Country Needs You Now," written with Rennie Cormack and G.B. McConnell, were two of the patriotic songs Al came up with, also in 1917.

The title of that last song proved prophetic for Al Dubin when he received a letter of "Greetings" from his local draft board. In September of 1917, Al found himself at Camp Upton in Yaphank, Long Island, a private in the 305th Field Artillery of the 77th Division, known as New York's own. The 77th Division not only cleared the Argonne Forest, but was the first National Army Division in Europe and the first National Army Division to be ordered to an active part of the line.

"So this is Yaphank," Al sighed as he brushed away the flies and mosquitoes and looked at row after row of wooden barracks. Al later compared the place to a boom town as he noted the civilian guards, sporting broad-brimmed hats, grey shirts and corduroy pants, packing pistols, Western fashion, and riding horses.

According to the History of the 77th Division, Camp Upton was indeed a special place.

The nascence and evolution of Camp Upton are truly remarkable. Within a month, the seemingly impossible was entered upon and accomplished, the construction of a city capable of housing 30,000 with the modern conveniences of electricity, metalled roads, and complete water and sewerage system. It was a triumph of efficiency made possible by the modern methods of construction, system and cooperation.

Entirely oblivious to the furore their expected arrival was creating at camp, those who were to have the honor of being the first arrivals had bid civilian life adieu and were assembled at the ferries and stations of New York and Brooklyn. Many carried large, highly expressive signs directing the Kaiser where he might best sojourn. Musical instruments of all sorts were brought along and many hip pockets bulged suspiciously. They were a motley crew; some had donned their best suits for the occasion, but the majority wore their oldest clothes. Every type was represented—the gunman and the gangster, the student and the clerk, the laborer and the loafer, the daily plodder, the lawyer. From the variety of languages spoken, one might have imagined himself at the Tower of Babel. These diverse types, accustomed to every condition of life, knowing for the most part no master, were to bow down before the military God, *Authority,* and emerge from the melting pot of training, an amalgamated mass of clear-thinking, clean-living men of whom America might well be proud.

Al Dubin did not emerge "clear-thinking and clean-living" from his Camp Upton experience, but he remembered it in later years with a great deal of nostalgia.

Though he always had a difficult time playing by the rules, Al never had any trouble making friends. It was also true at Camp Upton.

He was issued a mess kit and blankets and assigned to a numbered bunk by the receiving officer, and was soon digging and shoveling and working along with the rest of them. For recreation, he played baseball.

"You won't be playing ball tomorrow, Al," Johnny the Greek (as Al referred to him), his new friend, told him.

"Why not?" asked Al.

"We get our shots today. Come on."

Al watched, surprised, as Johnny the Greek and Irish Mike fainted at the sight of the needle. Al got his shots, ate his and Johnny's rations, and returned to his ballgame. He couldn't understand what all the fuss was about. Why be afraid of a needle? He was, after all, a doctor's son.

The budding songwriter was proud of his new status as a private in the United States Army and invited his father and young brother, Joe, for a weekend tour of Camp Upton, explaining to them he was now being initiated into the mysteries of firing a rifle.

Joe Dubin was impressed with his big brother in the uniform of a soldier and Al basked in the warmth of his admiring kid brother. It was good, Al thought, to have someone admire what he was doing, even if he had not chosen the "doing." Simon was disapproving of war and violence, but he hoped that army discipline might do for his son what he could not do; put some order into Al's life.

Al mastered the mysteries of a rifle. He blazed away with the rest of the Field Artillery on the 3,000 yard range in the wilderness surrounding the camp. Maneu-

vers were held daily and mimic battles waged in a trench system, constructed by the Engineers.

On his first weekend pass, Al went to the Majestic Theater in New York City to catch a show that he heard boasted six musical acts. One of the last acts, entitled "The Stowaway," was a combined musical and comedy act, featuring two men and a girl. Al thought the singing and harmonizing were superb. And the girl! She was a dream, a classic beauty with milk-white skin, long blond hair and incredible cornflower blue eyes. Al knew he had to meet her. But he had arranged to meet friends after the show and he had to catch the 2:59 a.m. "Owl" train back to Camp Upton so he would not be AWOL. So he noted her name on the program—McClay—and left the following note with the stage doorman.

> Dear Miss (I hope!) McClay:
> You have the most beautiful contralto voice I have ever heard. I write songs (lyrics) and I would be truly honored to have you render any one of them. Your beautiful voice is matched only by your beautiful face.
>
> Respectfully yours,
>
> Private Al Dubin,
> Camp Upton

Helen McClay did, for better or for worse for the both of them, respond to his note. And the two of them met in Al's publishing office, where Helen was warned by Al's peers not to go out with a man of his reputation.

Al learned that Helen had been married to one Ralph Kitner, who was still a part of her act of Kitner, Hawksley and McClay, and that she had a five-year-old daughter named Marie April. She was seeking an

annulment of her marriage to Kitner on grounds that she had not officially married him in the Catholic Church. She was also unofficially engaged to an actor named Bob Barrat.

None of these facts daunted Al. She was quite the loveliest lady he had ever seen, he told all his friends. She was the Madonna, the princess, the fantasy all rolled into one. For the first time in his life he was in love.

But the relationship had hardly begun when rumors were flying about Camp Upton that they would soon be sailing for France. Al was excited, a bit frightened of the unknown, but it never occurred to him that he would not return with all his limbs and faculties intact.

In April of 1918, Al Dubin sailed on the *Von Steuben* for France. It was a rough voyage and Al remembered that most of the men were sick a good deal of the time. Al was one of the few who didn't get seasick, so was kept busy cleaning up the vomit from bunks and decks.

"Bother me? Of course it didn't bother me," he said. "I got to eat my rations and their rations, too!"

They reached Brest on May 4 and debarked on May 6, where they found the big stone fort of Pontenazian Barracks, an old Napoleonic garrison. Al was fascinated and learned from one of the officers that the place had once been a monastery, and at another time a prison. Though the buildings were very damp and gloomy inside, Al noticed that many fruit trees blossomed within the walls. There was a rumor that Napoleon's ghost walked about at night but Al decided the noise was not Napoleon but the king-sized rats that inhabited the place.

Al spent the Fourth of July of 1918 parading in Bordeaux with the long rumbling, clanking column of guns and caissons in the greatest assemblage of artillery that most men had ever seen. The U.S. troops, escorted by the French infantry, moved through the city and pretty French girls lined the streets and balconies, showering them with flowers.

That night, Al practiced his limited French. His phrases, if not erudite, were at least practical. "Je t'aime." "Voulez-vous coucher avec moi?" If the lady said, "Oui," it was, "C'est bonne." If she slapped his face, it was, "C'est la guerre; c'est la vie."

That night, Greek Johnny, Irish Mike and Al paid a reluctant Frenchman to get them a half-dozen potatoes from his root cellar. They roasted them over an open fire and washed them down with cognac.

"One of the better feasts in my life," Al recalled. "Even though those potatoes had no butter, cream or seasonings, they were the best I ever tasted. They were black and charred on the outside, but moist and white and delicious when you broke them open. I could have eaten a dozen all by myself!"

In the army, Al learned to salute, to load a cannon, but that famous army discipline that is rumored to "make a man out of you" just didn't get through to the songwriter.

As always, Al continued to make many friends in the army and a particularly close friend was a man named Johnny who "worked" the big cannon with him.

His friend was killed, blown to bits by a grenade, while Al looked on.

"I wasn't frightened, not at all. I didn't want to run away or hide. I didn't really even feel sad, just empty,

standing there in the lousy mud. I kept thinking I would gladly get blown to bits if I could just have a hot bath first. At that moment, I really didn't even give a damn who won or lost the war."

My father rarely shared such feelings with me and I was more frightened than comprehending when he told me this in answer to the child's classic "What-did-you-do-in-the-war-Daddy?" question.

"But, Daddy, you never told me about that. You always talk about those funny things that happened to you in the war."

"Sure, Patrish, you talk about the funny things and you laugh a lot so you won't have to think about the pain of how it really was. If you did," he hesitated, groping for words to make me understand, "if you did, it would be too hard to just go on getting up every day and working."

I was awed. My father was a human being, always a novel discovery for a child. But that serious, thoughtful side didn't come out of the shadows very often. Al, the raconteur, amused and delighted an audience of one or twelve with his World War I stories.

The "train story" was one of his favorites. Al and a group of "doughboys" were on furlough and had taken seats on a French train, where they were eating hard bread, soft cheese and pouring down cognac. An attractive young woman sat across from them as they drunkenly told blue jokes, punctuated sentences with obscenities and commented crudely about the physical attributes of the young woman and how they could best be utilized by the doughboys. Al, mellow with cognac and laughter, feeling expansive, indicated to the woman

that they would share cheese, bread and cognac with her.

She got the non-verbal message, smiled demurely and said, in perfect English, "No, thank you. I have brought a lunch of my own."

Al Dubin blushed and they all sobered up fast!

Then there was Al's "horse" story. Having grown up in Philadelphia, Al had seen a horse or two and knew they had four legs and a tail, but that was about the extent of his knowledge. So when his commanding officer ordered him to deliver a message to a battle station some twenty kilometers away and indicated he should do this on horseback, Al rationally explained that he did not know how to mount or ride a horse.

"Dubin, get the hell on the fuckin' horse or I'll have you court-marshalled!"

"Yes, sir."

He mounted, backwards, rode about eight feet and was thrown in the mud.

The commanding officer, furious and frustrated, told him there was just no one else available to deliver the message, which was urgent, and he would just have to run the twenty kilometers.

"Run, Goddamn you! Run the message. Do you hear? Get going, now!"

Running was something Al did well and so he started, intending to pace himself, but he felt so terrible about the horse incident, so humiliated, that he decided he would run the distance without pacing himself and exert a superhuman effort to deliver the message.

In his mind, he saw the commendation: "For heroic service, above and beyond the call of duty, Private

Alexander Dubin, 77th Division, is awarded, etc. . . ."
The fantasy grew vague as exhaustion set in. He
dropped in his tracks, intending to sleep forty winks,
but he woke up twenty-four hours later. It was too late
to deliver the message.

The captain, one of the few people in his life who
didn't like Al, tried to have him dishonorably discharged but Dr. Simon Dubin appealed to an old friend
and patient who was a high-ranking officer, and Al received an honorable discharge from the United States
Army in 1918.

Though he got no medals during the war for his
horsemanship or his promptness in delivering mes-
sages, he wrote a song he was proud of and which received wide acclaim from the men with whom he
served. He titled it "They Didn't Think We'd Do It, But
We Did." Written with composer Fred Rath, published
by the 77th Division Association, the patriotic song cli-
maxed a show staged to entertain the troops. This is
where Al was really needed.

But he was sent to the front lines again. A gas attack
was imminent and all were issued gas masks. Sometime
during the attack, Al felt as if he were suffocating from
the mask and ripped it off, gulping in the poison gas.
His lungs were permanently damaged. For the rest of
his life, he fought a yearly bout with pneumonia and
frequently coughed up blood, alarming his wife. "It's
nothing," he would say, "just a little beet juice."

At discharge time, the army doctors told Al he was tu-
bercular and he should spend the next year or so of his
life at a sanitarium being treated for the disease.

So Al decided to live it up in preparation for a year or
two of what he would consider a boring life. He and a

friend rented a boat, found two willing women, bought a couple of cases of whiskey for this last fling. After two weeks of too much booze, food and sex, Al felt marvelous. When he went home to Philadelphia, his father examined him, assuring him he did not have tuberculosis, but that his lungs had, indeed, been damaged and he would have to be careful for the rest of his life.

"You are digging your grave with your teeth, both you and your brother. You must learn to control all your appetites or you will die a young man. You have a good, strong body, but you must take care of it," Simon admonished him. Fruitlessly.

Though Simon had taken care of himself, emotional stress from the divorce put too much of a strain on his weak heart, and he confided to a colleague after delivering a baby that he had but a year to live. His prediction fell short by only three months. Dr. Dubin died of a heart attack at his home on Girard Avenue on October 15, 1919. He was fifty-three years old.

Al, at twenty-eight, was devastated by the loss of his father, seeing in Simon's death the death of his own youth. He mourned his loss and denied his loss at the same time and tried, as usual, to run from the pain. On the way to the burial plot with his young brother, Joe, and the widow, Esther, Al jumped out of the limousine when it stopped for a signal, leaving the others to see Simon's remains laid to rest at the Jewish Cemetery Har-Nebo in Philadelphia.

One of those in the limousine was the blue-eyed blonde named Helen McClay, his dream girl, who had only recently become Al's bride.

FOUR

HELEN MCCLAY had written Al overseas, sent him gifts through the Red Cross, thought about the good-looking, rather unkempt, strange man, two years her junior, who wrote such romantic lyrics. Actually, they had very little in common except that they were both connected with the music business and they were both very lonely people.

But their tastes were worlds apart. When Al invited Helen out for a late after-theater supper, she would order a bowl of cornflakes and hot tea while Al's idea of a festive supper was shad roe and champagne, or at least lots of food and lots of liquor, though not necessarily in that order.

Helen, a devout Roman Catholic of Scotch-Irish-English ancestry, had been supporting herself and her mother and sisters and brother since she was nine years old. Her father had died when she was five years old and her mother invested unwisely the money that interior decorator John McClay had left his widow and

their four children. Helen's mother, Ellen Foley McClay, had been convent educated and could sew a fine seam, but that could not support her brood. So little Helen, with her bright good looks, pleasing singing voice, dancing talent, became the support of the family when Gus Edwards offered Ellen McClay's nine-year-old daughter a job and a chance for a show business career.

When Al returned from overseas, he was still enchanted with Helen's beauty. His "Irish girl" was what he called her. The lonely bard of Broadway began to dream about a home of his own, a wife to care for him, children. Still, he was wary. Many women had wanted to marry him as his earning capacity increased. Helen was earning over $300 a week, so Al hardly thought she needed his support. Still, he was wary.

If Al was not the trusting type, Helen was even less so. Her unfortunate liaison with a man ten years her senior had been a shattering emotional experience. Though Helen loved and respected Ralph Kitner and continued to be part of his act, they fought violently over her Catholicism. Ralph, with a strong Protestant background, the son of a physician who had disapproved of his son's show business career, was firmly anti-Catholic and refused to allow Marie April to be brought up in the Catholic faith. So Helen left him, believing in her heart that it was more important for her daughter to be raised a Roman Catholic than it was for her to have a father in the home.

So Al and Helen, each already bruised by misfortunes, each looking unrealistically for the other to make up for deprivations of the past, began to keep steady company, a unique experience for Al.

To impress his Helen, Al hired a car one Sunday afternoon so they could take a ride in the country. Since Helen didn't like any of Al's favorite bars or restaurants, he thought she would enjoy a ride to Connecticut. They ran out of gas. The driver apologized and said he would walk back to the nearest station to buy gas. It was winter and by five o'clock, dusk had fallen. Helen was frightened that this man, whom she realized she hardly knew, was going to rape her. Perhaps he had paid the driver to run out of gas? Al was being a bit affectionate, but he was just trying to pass the time until the driver returned.

As five o'clock turned into six o'clock and the man didn't return, Al began to have doubts about Helen. Al Dubin always carried huge amounts of cash on his person (when he had it) and that winter's night was no exception. He had four or five hundred dollars in his pocket. Perhaps Helen McClay knew that. Perhaps she had bribed the driver of the car and they were in this together? Perhaps she planned that Al would fall asleep and the driver would come back, overpower him and steal his money.

The driver eventually returned and they were both safely returned to Manhattan, neither of them the worse for wear.

Five weeks later, even though the annulment had not been granted yet, Al Dubin and Helen McClay became man and wife in the office of a Justice of the Peace in New York City. Though Helen's love for the songwriter proved temporarily stronger than her religious ties, she planned to marry him in the Church as soon as the annulment came through. She also had plans to convert the Jewish man into a Catholic gentleman.

When Al took Helen home to Philadelphia, Simon and Al's new wife formed an instant and mutual liking and respect for one another. Helen, being uneducated herself, was always in awe of a college graduate and placed doctors on a pedestal second only to priests.

Simon, in his turn, was glad that Al had gone outside the ranks of Jewish women and picked a Gentile, believing in his own eugenics theory that it was good for the human species not to "inbreed."

Helen often remembered in later years what Dr. Dubin had said to her:

"I am so happy that my son married a healthy beautiful Irish girl who has already demonstrated her ability to bear a healthy child. There has been no intermarriage in my family or Alick's mother's family—ever. And it is about time to introduce new, fresh stock. Eastern European Jews are too inbred. This is a real honor for us to have you join the family. I look forward to having a grandchild and I wish you two would hurry up. I have not much time left. My grandchild should be strong and healthy coming from Jewish and Irish stock. Good for the race that you two have found each other."

Helen saw where Al got his charm! She was enchanted with Simon and with his warmth, compassion and concern for his fellow humans. Though she knew him for only a few months, she felt a great loss at his death.

Minna Dubin was not quite so cordial. In fact, Minna was appalled that her adored firstborn son would marry a "shiksa" and very undiplomatically told Helen so. She also proclaimed her total disbelief in Simon's speculative eugenics theory, stating he had no proof of "such nonsense."

Angrily, Helen responded that Al had never been exposed to Judaism as a religion so why should it matter if he married a Gentile? Also, she pointed out to Minna, undiplomatically, that she intended to convert Al to Catholicism, and then they would have a Catholic church wedding.

"Convert to Catholicism?" screamed Minna, who spoke with a strong accent. "That is ridiculous! That is like holding up a chicken and saying, 'This is a fish.' That is no fish because someone says so—a chicken will always be a chicken, no matter how many people call it a fish. Alick will always be a Jew, no matter how many of your priests call him a Catholic!"

Brother Joe didn't share his mother's feelings. He fell in love with the beautiful Helen just as his big brother had done. In fact, when Al was courting Helen, young Joseph formally asked "Miss Helen" for a date one evening, after first consulting his coin purse to see if he could afford to take her out. Gently, she turned the boy down. Being such a beautiful woman, she was used to the adulation and admiration of the opposite sex.

After a short honeymoon in Albany, New York, Helen and Al Dubin settled down in an apartment in Manhattan with Marie April. Al was very fond of his new daughter and loved taking her to sporting events. Helen didn't share his interest in spectator sports any more than she shared his interest in whiskey or food. She didn't even like to cook!

So Al and little Marie attended football games, baseball games, bike races, went to Coney Island. He encouraged Marie to take up athletics in school as she had a real talent for running and jumping, and he was exceedingly proud of her when she won a broadjumping

event, telling all his friends with obvious fatherly pride. It was as if he were reliving his own sports-filled youth at Perkiomen Seminary. Having a child was a terrific thing, he decided.

But Al wanted a son; a daughter couldn't, after all, play football. So when Helen announced she was pregnant, there was rejoicing in the Dubin household. Helen's pregnancy was uneventful, but she began experiencing labor pains two months before term. She was not worried, as Marie April had been a seventh-month, two-pound baby and had survived.

Al, the prototype of the nervous father, paced the hospital corridor after a taxi had rushed them both to the hospital. Al was ecstatic when Dr. William Haynes found him and spoke the magic words, "It's a boy!" However, he quickly added that, though Helen was in good shape, the baby was only four pounds and very, very frail. His birth wail had been a weak one, the doctor explained.

"But Helen's first child was only two pounds and she lived. Get another doctor, get a wet nurse, do something. They saved little Marie in Boston. Why can't you make my son strong here in New York?"

Al was becoming belligerent, but the doctor understood his concern. Al asked the doctor for a sedative to calm his nerves and then went in to see Helen. She was full of fear that their son would not live, but Al assured her that all was well and that Simon Joseph (to be called Joe) would grow up to be the best damn quarterback at Fordham University.

Four days later, Simon Joseph Dubin died. Helen cried in her hospital bed alone because her husband had gone off to celebrate and they could not locate him

to tell him the sad news. Dr. Haynes and her sister, Ethel, who was caring for Marie April, lent their support to Helen in her time of need, trying to make up for a husband's neglect. She told her sister she hoped there would be no more children.

When they finally found Al and told him the news he stopped celebrating and started drinking twice as much in an effort to saturate the pain he felt—the pain and the melodramatic self-pity. He was seldom home during this period, and when he *was* home he would tell Helen that if only his son had lived he would not feel the need to drink so much.

Helen was confused, hurt, angry. She nagged and berated him when he did come home. The marriage was in real trouble and both felt bitter and disillusioned. But Helen did not want to admit defeat. She felt once Al became a Catholic, all would be well. She kept pressing and Al seemed genuinely interested in the Christian philosophy.

The Christian concept of gently "turning the other cheek" appealed to Al who did not like the Biblical "eye for an eye and a tooth for a tooth." The Rabbi Jesus was to him a radical revolutionary with a dynamic concept of brotherhood.

So it was not too difficult for the songwriter to convert to Catholicism when he believed that Catholicism was a natural evolvement from Judaism. Memories of Mary, the kind and loving Polish nursemaid, had stayed with him always; he wanted very much to please his new wife, and, finally, there was Father Goldberg.

Father Joseph Goldberg, a Jew who had converted to Catholicism, was an ordained priest who possessed a brilliant and enquiring mind and popular music was his

avocation. So Goldberg and Dubin had more than a little in common. To make the relationship complete, the priest had a fondness for Mt. Vernon rye whiskey, Al's favorite drink. Often, they went out on the town (Father Goldberg turning his Roman collar around), raised their glasses and exchanged stories, discussing literature, philosophy and celibacy until three or four in the morning. Helen never minded when Al came home drunk after being with Father Goldberg. After all, Al had been with a priest, and as far as Helen was concerned, a priest, drunk or sober, could do no wrong.

It was Father Goldberg who baptized Al after he had completed his instructions. No one explained to Al that during his baptism he would have a small amount of water poured over his head. He thought he was going to have to climb in the baptismal font that could accommodate maybe a seven-pound infant. He was about to chicken out and leave the ceremony when Father Goldberg grabbed his arm and poured water over his head. The Jewish gentleman from Philadelphia was now a Roman Catholic.

Shortly after his baptism, Helen was granted an annulment of her first marriage and she married Al in the Church on March 19, 1921, at the Church of St. Elizabeth in New York City. Father John E. Wickam was the officiating priest and the witnesses were John J. O'Brien and Ethel Mooney, Helen's sister from Philadelphia. Both Al and Helen celebrated the occasion, for they believed their marriage was now "blessed" by God and by the Catholic Church. Because of Al's recent baptism, according to Catholic teaching, his soul was now free of all past sins and, because of this, Helen earnestly and naïvely believed that their basic problems

were solved. With all due respects to the lady, she failed to take into consideration that the Church might clean up a person's past act—it was not a guarantee for the future.

Helen's sister, Ethel, was happy for her, believing she was a lucky lady to have captured so fine a gentleman as Al Dubin. Ethel never changed her mind about Al; she always looked forward to his visits to her and her family; never spoke a condemning word about her brother-in-law, no matter what he did; viewed him as a very talented and loving man who brought joy and pleasure to thousands with his lyrics. Though Ethel was as devout in her Catholicism as her sister Helen, she believed in a God who would forgive Al almost anything because of his contributions. It was to be Ethel, many years after she witnessed the marriage, who was to accompany Al's casket on his last grim journey from New York to California.

The year he married, Al collaborated with Paul Cunningham and Charles Edmonds on "Sundown Brings Back Memories of You," which appeared in *The Greenwich Village Follies,* and also turned out some special material for the show. He was full of good resolutions now that he was an even more married man!

Because Prohibition was a law of the land, Helen thought the drinking problem would be no more. She truly believed that life with Al would be smooth sailing from now on and left her vaudeville job to become a full-time wife and mother.

Things didn't quite work out the way she planned; there had been no magic in either the conversion to Catholicism or the church wedding to change these two people who had so little in common, who came from

such diverse backgrounds and who had such different expectations of marriage. Prohibition proved no deterrent to Al's drinking, but succeeded in compounding his problems when he befriended members of New York's underworld, partially to assure himself a steady supply of good booze, partially to know when and where there was an available poker game or a reliable bookie, and partially for the excitement of it. Al thrived on excitement and when there wasn't any, he created some. Another considerable attraction of the underworld was that it helped sustain his image of "bad guy" on the verge of disaster. Involvement with questionable people, welching on gambling debts, drinking too much too often was an excellent way to play the disaster game.

Both Helen and Al were, in their own ways, trying. Helen began taking a real interest in his work, offering comments on his lyrics. She made the mistake of criticizing one line and Al left in a huff. When he returned, he told her there was a new organization, founded by Victor Herbert, called the American Society of Composers, Authors and Publishers (ASCAP). ASCAP would act as a licensing agent for songs played and authors, composers, publishers would receive revenue from the use of their songs. ASCAP would also continue as an estate after the death of the member. It sounded like a great organization to Helen, but Al procrastinated. Helen nagged and Al was accepted in ASCAP in 1921.

That same year, he rented a small office in downtown Manhattan with some colleagues where they were to form their own publishing firm. Even Al, with his frightful lack of business acumen, realized that the pub-

lishers, not the authors or composers, received the lion's share of money from a successful song.

Helen was thrilled. Al had a place to go to work every day, just like an ordinary man. She set about collecting sheet music of his songs to decorate the walls. Months later, it was an attractive, cozy office with all of Al's songs up on the walls. Helen was very proud of the job she had done.

But Al had a disagreement with his partners and walked out of the partnership, leaving all the sheet music on the walls. When Helen went back to retrieve the copies, the office had been vacated and all the music was gone! She never saved another one of Al's songs—even when he was turning out hits every year in Hollywood.

They fought about money. To hear Al tell it, Helen had made a pauper out of him. To hear Helen tell it, Al didn't give her enough money for a quart of milk. The truth probably lay somewhere in between.

Money was not the only area of disagreement in those early days of the marriage. Helen's fears grew and her anger escalated as Al's drinking bouts, some lasting for days, continued. Al did not recognize his compulsion to drink as an illness and neither did his wife. He expected to continue his old lifestyle of sleeping until four or five in the afternoon and, unrealistically, expected the household to conform to his schedule. Helen, on the other hand, thought her life and Marie's should continue in a normal pattern with no consideration for a hung-over husband. Dinner was to be served at six every evening. She was not a flexible woman.

So, tight-lipped and angry, Helen went about her household tasks, longing for less complicated days as a professional entertainer, while Al raged if Helen or

Marie made any noise that awakened him. Al was not noted for his temper unless someone woke him up unexpectedly. Then, watch out!

In addition to constant squabbling about money and drinking, Al became increasingly disillusioned with his Helen. She was not the dream girl he had fantasized and he couldn't forgive her for that. Helen was no more sensitive to his needs than his mother had been.

Helen's qualities that had at first appealed to Al were fast turning into liabilities. Originally, he was enchanted with the idea that she drank only "sasparilla," shunning alcohol totally. But as Helen became increasingly shrewish about Al's drinking habits, he began to wish she would tie one on with him, so she could understand his need. He figured if she were busy with her own hangover, she wouldn't be concerned so much with his.

Unlike his mother, Minna, Helen was a domestic creature, enjoying keeping house, decorating and sewing. But her sewing took time away from him and his needs and she was always changing the furniture around. One night when he almost broke a leg tripping over a new furniture arrangement in the dark, he decided her domesticity wasn't all that appealing. Al Dubin now regretted his hasty decision to marry.

NO ONE WAS OVERJOYED when Helen announced she was again with child. Helen hoped it would prove to be glue for a faltering marriage. But things were too torn by then to be mended, and my birth on November 26, 1922, worked an additional hardship on the relationship. The domestic routine, Helen's growing and ill-disguised hostility, her constant complaints, a wailing and ailing infant, a school-aged adopted daughter proved too much for Al. He took off when I was six weeks old. But not before losing out in an argument with Helen to name the baby "Broadway." When she reacted with horror at his choice, he suggested a more conservative "Roberta," but she finally settled for Helen Patricia—Helen for her and Patricia for the Princess Pat Regiment in Canada that Helen had entertained both before and after they went overseas to fight the Hun.

So, though his daughter might have been "Broadway" in Al's mind, he soon had a child that everyone called "Patti."

Al left Helen with no financial resources and she set about, unsuccessfully, to find him. In desperation, she moved her new baby and Marie to her brother's home on Long Island.

Where did Al Dubin go? When asked, he would respond with different stories.

"I went to Philadelphia, got a room and took a job tending bar on Race Street." (He did, indeed, once work as a bartender on Race Street, the skid row area of Philadelphia, but when, no one knows for sure.)

"I suffered an attack of amnesia and shipped out with the Merchant Marine."

"I was busy writing lyrics, night and day, to earn money for the family."

At any rate, repentant and feeling guilty after a few months, Al claimed his family from Johnny McClay's home and everybody was back together in an apartment in Washington Heights.

Songwriter Jimmy McHugh, another Irishman Al dearly loved, was a frequent visitor at this period—eating dinner with the family, playing with the baby, working with Al. Occasionally, they even signed "the pledge" together. (The pledge was a promise to give up alcohol.) The pledge never quite took for Al. The scene at this time was one of domesticity—troubled domesticity.

Helen cautiously bought a few items of furniture. Al invited friends over for all-night poker games. Helen couldn't sleep because of the noise and when she complained Al took to playing poker elsewhere.

In 1923 Al wrote a song with Joe Garren and Fred Rath entitled "Broadway," foreshadowing his future

Academy Award-winning "Lullaby of Broadway," and, again, lost a plea to Helen to name me "Broadway."

"No one would ever forget her with a name like that!" he argued.

"That's what I'm afraid of," my mother replied. "They could call her 'Broad' for short!" And that evidently ended the argument.

Two songs Al wrote that year reflected his personal life—"Unhappy," written with Joe Burke, and another Burke and McHugh tune, "If You Know Her Side of the Story," reflecting the empathy he felt for his wife in compassionate moments. He collaborated with Billy Rose on the lyrics of "Chattachoochee," the melody of which was composed by an up-and-coming tunesmith by the name of Sammy Fain.

Nineteen twenty-four marked a year of herculean effort for Al Dubin. He turned over a new leaf; he went on the wagon and settled down to working on a more or less steady basis, publishing thirty-one songs, four of which were renderings of classics. One song published that year with music by Jimmy McHugh was entitled "My Kid." It was written to honor Al's new daughter and Jimmy's new son.

Jack Mills published another Dubin song in 1925 entitled "Waters of the Perkiomen," music by F. Henri Klickman. It's not too easy to find a rhyme for Perkiomen, but Al used "foeman" and "gloamin.' " After all, he wrote the song to prove a point to Reverend Kriebel, the man who had expelled him.

Milt Hagen was Director of Exploitation at Jack Mills Publishing and Al saw to it that he wrote Kriebel to tell

him about the new waltz. (The "new" waltz is still being sung by Perkiomen students today.)

Kriebel took the bait:

> I wish you would send me several copies of the song. I am very much interested to know the whereabouts of Al Dubin. Can you tell me? I am anxious to know whether this waltz was written lately or whether it was published some time already. Mr. Dubin has real ability to write songs. Our school song was written by him.

Al read the reply and laughingly explained to Hagen that "the bastards threw me out of the school fourteen years ago." He refused to let Hagen give Kriebel his home address, so Kriebel wrote the following letter to Al Dubin.

> My dear Dubin:
> I want to tell you how much we appreciate your song, "Waters of the Perkiomen," and it pleases us to know that you still remember the old school and community. It is also very gratifying that you had your publisher favor us with two copies of the song. We are going to have it mimeographed and soon every student will know the words, and we hope to sing it frequently in chapel. They expect to feature the song at the Aurora Theatre up in town this evening. The Perkiomen Symphony Orchestra, together with the organ will play it, and our Librarian, Miss Kneule, will sing it. One of the members of our Faculty, Prof. Roeder, will make a short address, explaining your connection with the school and kind remembrance of it.
> By unanimous vote, the Faculty and students send congratulations to you and best wishes.
> I should be very glad to hear from you and I hope I may have the pleasure of meeting you some time

in New York when I get over there on school business."

When Al read the letter he didn't know whether to gloat, get mad or cry. So he got drunk. So much for the water wagon.

In addition to the publication of "Waters of the Perkiomen" in 1925, another significant event occurred in the professional life of Al Dubin. He met Harry Warren, who was to become his future collaborator at Warner Brothers. These two men were as different from each other as champagne and soda water. But they did have one big thing in common—they were both pros, talented and dedicated to their craft.

The feisty, friendly, warm, Italian Harry was a family man. Al was a loner once again, separated temporarily from Helen, with his nose pressed against the glass of other people's lives. So he was pleased when Harry invited him to his home in Forest Hills for dinner after they had met, quite by accident, at the Oyster Bar in Grand Central Station. So the two men who were to give the music world some of the biggest Hollywood musical hits started their relationship discussing oysters, not words and music.

Al charmed Harry's beautiful, red-haired wife, praising her lavishly for the roast pork dinner she served him. When Al Dubin paid a compliment, he made it sound like Shakespeare's Sonnets to the Dark Lady. He had the knack, talent, of convincing the person on the receiving end of the compliment that he or she had just done something no other mortal could possibly do in just that unique way—whether it was cooking a roast pork dinner, sewing a dress, writing a terrific lyric, or composing a beautiful melody. It was a

magic he managed to weave that made his faults shrink to insignificance in the eyes of those who loved him.

During this period, Al and Harry wrote their first tune together, which didn't exactly make musical history. It was titled "Too Many Kisses in the Summer Bring Too Many Tears in the Fall."

But another song published that same year was a hit. Titled "A Cup of Coffee, a Sandwich and You," the lyric was written in conjunction with Billy Rose, who then found Joseph Meyer to put a melody to the catchy title. According to Joe Meyer, the title was Al's, as were most of the lines in the song. Al's inspiration was Omar Khayyam's *Rubaiyat* which contained the classic line: *A loaf of bread, a jug of wine and thou . . .*." The song, sung in *Charlot's Revue* by Gertrude Lawrence and Jack Buchanan, was a favorite of Al's and he hustled singers of the day to perform his song. Indulging in one of his favorite hobbies, lunch, at Dinty Moore's one afternoon, he spotted vaudeville performer Nick Lucas and asked him to sing the song. Nick agreed and noted Al's usual sloppy appearance—wrinkled suit coat, stained shirt, ill-fitting pants.

Nick noted, to his surprise, years later, when Al had gone to Hollywood to work for Warner Brothers, that all this had changed.

"He came backstage to see me and wish me well. Was I surprised! He was still too fat but, instead of an ill-fitting, spotted, wrinkled suit, his was beautifully tailored, of expensive material. He looked very sharp. And I told him so. He was like a shy, pleased kid when I complimented him and brushed it off as if he were too embarrassed to talk about it."

Lucas also recalled Al's blowing smoke in his face from his Havana cigars and used to complain to the songwriter. When Al wrote "Tiptoe Through the Tulips with Me," which Lucas recorded and made famous, he said to Nick: "This might not make you too happy, Nick, but that song 'Tiptoe' is going to buy me an awful lot of Havana cigars."

Though Al, indeed, looked sloppy on occasions, it was of the utmost importance to him that he smoke the most expensive cigars, drink premium whiskey and leave the largest tips.

Towards the end of his life, when he was down on his luck in Hollywood, he would not go to his favorite barber in Hollywood because he could not afford to give him a generous tip. His wife, Helen, scoffed at him for such an attitude, but Al held fast. "No, tip; no shave."

Shortly after "A Cup of Coffee, a Sandwich and You," Al penned another lyric—on the back of an old gas bill envelope—and he entitled it "Among My Souvenirs." He was in debt at this time, needed quick cash to get a small stake in a poker game and sold that lyric to one Edgar Leslie, for $25.00. It became one of the biggest hits of the day, earning a small fortune for the publishers and generous royalties for Leslie, but Al's name has never appeared on the lyric. Dubin sold many lyrics in the same fashion for $5 or $50 but he only brooded about "Among My Souvenirs" because it went on to become such a big hit.

He turned his hand to writing a book, again to earn quick money. He contracted with Mills Music Co. to write a book on how to write songs and though they gave him several months to write it, he did not begin to work on it until the night before the due date. He

worked on it through the night and at dawn he had finished writing *The Art of Songwriting,* which claimed to contain a "wealth of information for amateur songwriters." The selling price was $1.00. Al was proud of that book, though he doubted it could help someone who didn't already have that elusive quality—talent, the ability to wed a lyric to a melody, that fine instinct to know what men and women, boys and girls wanted to say to each other with their songs. It was Dubin's belief that sheet music, which accounted for the bulk of song sales in the twenties, was purchased by females between the ages of fifteen and twenty-five. Consequently, he keyed his lyrics to that segment of the population unless he was writing special material for a show or nightclub act.

Though Al Dubin was doing well professionally in the twenties, his home life was erratic. He was a now-you-see-him-now-you-don't husband and father. He continued to squabble with his wife over the same old things. Every so often, Helen would threaten to leave and he would tell her to go right ahead but not to expect any money from him. She wasn't getting much money from him as it was and she decided she would have to go back to work to secure a steady source of income. She found a job modelling hats in a small millinery store on Fifth Avenue. She had worked there only two days when I developed a severe case of pneumonia.

Helen was frightened. She needed and wanted her husband to share the responsibility for decisions to be made regarding a sick child but she didn't know where to find Al. Dr. Charles Haynes had told her that hospitalization was a necessity, not a choice, and he could not be responsible for my recovery if I remained at home.

Helen called some of Al's friends, though she knew so few of them, and she called publisher Irving Mills. She tried to retain her dignity as she talked to Mills, tried to hide the fact that she had not seen her husband for a couple of weeks. Finally, she gave up, called a taxi and took me to the hospital for admission.

Several days later, just as I had developed a severe case of measles and hospital officials were demanding I leave the hospital because they were not equipped to handle contagious diseases, Al strolled nonchalantly into the apartment. Helen was literally and figuratively wringing her hands because Dr. Haynes had said that to move me would cost me my life. She didn't even scream at Al for his disappearance though she did manage to turn a few screws in the guilt machine.

Al could act in a crisis—when the crisis involved another. He contacted his friend Jimmy Walker, mayor of New York City. Al had met Walker in 1905 when the two teenagers were hanging out on Tin Pan Alley. Al told the mayor he still sang Walker's song, "Will You Love Me in December as You Do in May?" when he had a few too many rock and ryes at a party.

Skillfully, dramatically, Al described the plight of his only child, weaving in the memories of twenty years ago when they were both struggling for recognition as lyricists.

Walker came through and I was allowed to remain hospitalized until I was completely well and Dr. Haynes discharged me.

Helen never tried to return to work after that incident. Mollified by the fact that Al had come through when she really needed him, she tried harder to accept him and his oftentimes unacceptable behavior. She

longed for less complicated days and spoke with nostalgia of her "nineteen years in show business," as if they had been the best years of her life.

Al had a difficult time trying to understand why Helen did not think he was "the greatest" when most of his friends did offer him psychological rewards for his thoughtful favors on their behalf. The songwriter was always willing to grant a favor for a friend and he asked no favors in return unless it was of the utmost importance.

Helen called on Al on another occasion when money was needed for an outstanding doctor's bill on my account. Al approached famous gambler Nicky Arnstein for a loan which Al repaid several months later. Al had lost so much money gambling in Arnstein's establishment that he didn't even consider the borrowed money a loan. "Reshuffled money," was what he called it.

The summer of 1927 found the Dubin family in Deal Beach on vacation. We had been there only a few hours when I managed to get myself bitten on the backside by a dog. Al and Helen rushed me to the doctor who treated me and said I could not swim for the next two weeks. Helen was all for packing up and going back to New York, but my father said "no" and took me instead for a train ride. I obviously could not sit but had to ride kneeling. He explained that any fool could sit on a train; it took some class and originality to ride backwards. He overwhelmed me with chocolate ice cream bars and funny stories. My father turned a big disappointment into an unexpected pleasure for me. He handled other people's crises in creative ways but could not manage to do the same for his own. Perhaps he was

waiting for someone, a counterpart of Al Dubin, to come along and do it for him.

Al Dubin enjoyed nothing better than to watch others enjoy themselves, especially when he had been a major contributor to that enjoyment. The greatest compliment you could pay the man (other than praising his lyrics) was to say: "I'm having the time of my life!" His green eyes would crinkle up and shine with pleasure at having set the stage for another's pleasure.

If Al rated an A-plus as a friend and as the "good guy" who delighted in another's joy, pleasure, success, he drew a D or an F on the domestic front with his lady. Though he was an understanding and sympathetic parent in many ways, he was not the most reliable of fathers. One weekend, when Helen travelled to Philadelphia to visit her sister, she left Al in charge of me and my sister. It was winter and there was a lot of snow on the ground. Helen cautioned Al not to let my sister Marie go sledding on the hill in front of our Adrian Avenue apartment. Al promised. But as soon as Helen was out the door, Al made a deal with Marie. He told her she could sled on the hill if she would babysit her little sister while he went to a ballgame. Marie accepted.

She had not been on the hill ten minutes when she was struck by a car and, though not seriously injured, she was terrified, bruised and cut about the face, making her injuries appear worse than they were. Al was in the bathroom when the police came to the door with Marie. He rushed to answer the bell, holding his pants in one hand, saw Marie, and let go of his pants. She started to cry, not because she was hurt but because she

was embarrassed to see her father standing there in his undershorts.

When Helen returned, there was a terrible row, much explaining on Al's part, tears from Marie, shouts and insults from both Al and Helen.

The next time Helen had occasion to visit her sister in Philadelphia, she took my sister and me with her. When she got home this time, the New York fire department was hosing down our apartment. It seemed Al had gotten hungry while she was gone, didn't want to brave the snow, and put a can of baked beans, unopened, in a 400-degree oven. Naturally, they exploded and there were beans on the kitchen ceiling for weeks afterward. Al Dubin was not a domestic man. Babysitting, cooking, driving a car and changing light bulbs remained deep mysteries for him that he never was able to solve.

While Al wasn't doing too well as cook or babysitter, he had been engaged for two Broadway shows in 1927—*White Lights* and *Take the Air*—and merited a couple of hits from his songs, "Heaven Help a Sailor on a Night Like This," written with friend Joe Burke, and "All By My Ownsome."

While he was working on the show, he and Helen had another violent disagreement about gambling, money and drinking and Al took off for the McAlpin Hotel in New York City from where he wrote me a letter on the occasion of my First Holy Communion. He and Helen were too furious at one another at the time for him to even attend the ceremony and it was at eight a.m.—a little early in the day for Al.

The letter read: "I am so proud of you, little sweetie. Keep your brand new playmate always in your heart. Love, Daddy."

It was those letters, those gifts, those special little attentions that Al Dubin so deftly employed that led others to forgive him his faults.

Alice Kahal, wife of the late songwriter Irving, was pleased and surprised to receive a case of ale while she was in the hospital, having given birth to a daughter. Someone had told Al that ale produced mother's milk and he signed his note to that effect. Alice never forgot his kindness.

One Christmas, when Al was in New York and the family was in California, he sent a beautiful card, along with the gifts, and signed the card, "Love from Papa, Daddy and Al"—our three titles for him. When I studied French in school, my birthday or Christmas card was a French one; when I studied Latin, a phrase in Latin closed his letters.

He carried his thoughtfulness, his care for those he loved, to extremes. On one memorable Fourth of July in Atlantic City when I was about four years old, the fireworks display so frightened me that I cried and asked my all-powerful father to do something. My mother had a difficult time talking him out of calling the mayor to demand that all fireworks cease because of one small child's fright. He had never learned to solve problems himself; he ran from them or "fixed" them; solving or working through a problem did not exist for him so he certainly was not in a position to teach anyone else how to solve one.

An exception to his lack of problem-solving ability occurred one summer in Atlantic City when Helen told him I was very sick, could not keep anything on my stomach, but she was sure orange juice would provide the magic cure. Orange juice was to Helen what chicken

soup was to her Jewish sisters. So at three a.m., Al walked to the local grocery store, tossed a rock through the window and stole a dozen oranges. The next afternoon he went to the store to pay for both the oranges and the broken window, basking in the glory of compliments that the clerks paid to him when they heard his story.

Al loved the drama of the incident. Here he had a chance to play "big Daddy"; shine as a hero in his wife's eyes, prove to a stranger that he was a loving father, a true family man.

No matter that he might leave the next day for a two-week binge with his gambling and drinking buddies where wife or child could not find him. This was *today* and this is how he perceived himself. And if Helen did not properly appreciate his heroic actions, then he could justify his disappearance, his drinking.

The decade of the twenties was drawing to a close. As my father had predicted, Herbert Hoover became president; the stock market crashed without his prediction, and Al ate his way through pounds of pickled pigs' feet and Kosher dill pickles. He marked with great interest the growth of radio broadcasting and the implications for a songwriter. He avidly read detective story magazines "to relax," recited Poe's "The Raven" dozens of times and taught me how to make rhymes.

THERE WAS TALK ON BROADWAY of a new era in Hollywood, that never-never land of perpetual sunshine. *The Jazz Singer* marked, of course, the advent of sound and sound meant singing as well as talking. Some studios were hiring big name singers and those singers had to have songs to sing. There was excitement on Tin Pan Alley.

Al Dubin, with four Broadway shows to his credit and several popular hits, was one of the first to board the Superchief after Warner Brothers purchased the publishing firms of Witmark, Remick and Harms. Dubin was under contract to Harms so Warner Brothers automatically fell heir to his services.

Al drank a lot, ate a lot and slept a lot as the train rolled West. He felt like a pioneer, coming to a strange land by way of Zurich, Philadelphia, New York. Maybe it wouldn't last; maybe it was just a "flash in the pan" (one of his favorite expressions). At any rate, he would have a steady salary, $500.00 per week, maybe some recognition. And the boys in the back room had told him the climate was great.

Al fell in love with Southern California as soon as his foot touched down at Glendale Station. No snow! He took one look at the palm trees, felt the warm sun and said, "This is for me!"

He hated snow and, uncharacteristically, perceived the reality of slush before the beauty of the snowflakes. Los Angeles—Hollywood—was Al's kind of town. As far as he could see, it had everything but good restaurants and that lack was soon remedied when he discovered San Francisco.

The songwriter rented a bachelor apartment in Hollywood, bought a spittoon for his studio office in Burbank and settled down to do what he was being paid to do—write lyrics. He wrote with Jimmy Monaco and M.K. Jerome but the bulk of his work was with his friend Joe Burke.

Al had always been prolific as a lyricist, but he was initially shocked by the casual attitude of his studio bosses when they asked for eight or ten songs, due in two weeks. In New York, Al had often spent two weeks, or longer, on one lyric. It wasn't going to be easy, but now his proficiency at turning out ideas would really pay off.

His partner, Joe Burke, didn't see how he could possibly compose eight melodies in two weeks. He felt it just couldn't be done. But Al tried to simmer down his friend, making light of the situation, telling jokes about the studio personnel, seeing the comic side of two harried men grasping for an idea, any idea to turn into a popular song.

It was 1929 and Warner Brothers was making *Gold Diggers of Broadway*. Dubin and Burke wrote the whimsical classic, "Tiptoe Through the Tulips with Me." No one at Warners was impressed. Al authored lyrics for

three other musicals—*Sally, Hold Everything* and *She Can't Say No.* He also supplied lyrics for the movie productions of *Evidence, Show of Shows* and *In the Headlines.*

Joe Burke was becoming increasingly worried that Warner Brothers would not renew his contract. The Depression was certainly not giving way to good economic times and the question was—how many songwriters would the studios need if they did not continue to turn out musicals?

As usual, Al sensed Joe's distress and tried to humor him out of it, pointing out that, even if they both got fired, they could break into vaudeville doing a comic version of "Tiptoe Through the Tulips with Me"—"all 450 graceful pounds of us," Al said.

"Can't you see us, Joe, in our little tutus, coming on in the final moments of the act, cavorting around with those gorgous skinny chorines?"

In spite of his worries, Joe had to laugh at the image of these two overweight songsmiths dancing to the strains of their hit song.

Al loved California more each day and was soon sending Helen postcards showing people swimming on the beach in Santa Monica in February. We were, of course, up to our ear muffs in slush. He wanted his family to come West. He would rent a house; he would buy a car, an object we had never owned. You had to have a car to get about here, he explained. The studio limousine had to pick him up every day to take him to work. My mother, perhaps, could fill him in on what was protocol in terms of artichokes. He had been served one at dinner in a Beverly Hills mansion and he didn't have the vaguest idea what to do with the damn thing!

So in 1929 the Dubin family moved West to start all over again with an infant industry—the Hollywood musical. It was a time of despair for most of America, with the Depression at its worst and no relief in sight. Jobs were either difficult or impossible to find. College graduates pumped gas or waited on tables for outrageously low wages.

For the Dubins, it was the exact opposite. Al was earning more than he had ever earned in his life, Helen had traded a cramped New York apartment for a house in Beverly Hills and my sister and I found every day an adventure as we walked the backlots of Warners, meeting real live stars and celebrities.

The personal hopes of the Dubins were high at this gloomy period of America's history. A nation in crisis had become the songwriter's golden opportunity. The musicals of the next decade probably helped almost as many people retain their sanity, their sense of perspective and of self, almost as much as did the innovative programs soon to be introduced by Franklin Delano Roosevelt. Dubin's lyrics combined with Harry Warren's great tunes and Busby Berkeley's "I don't-believe what-I'm-seeing" production numbers helped many people forget about the grimness of unemployment, overdue bills and unpaid rent, if only for an hour. People could laugh at themselves in a therapeutic way, seeing the humor, black though it was, in certain aspects of the Great Depression. The musical was about to become an art form, an indelible part of a growing nation's history. Ruby Keeler, Dick Powell, Busby Berkeley and Dubin and Warren were about to make Hollywood musical history. If life is truly a matter of timing, Al Dubin made his Hollywood entrance right on cue.

In 1930, with the family settled in a rented bungalow in Beverly Hills, both his daughters in school, an Essex in the garage, Al authored lyrics for Joe Burke's tunes for the following musicals: *Life of the Party* (which was never produced), *The Cuckoos, Oh Sailor Beware* and *Top Speed*.

The thirties! There was an air of naïveté to go with the times. Happy days were here, or, if not, just around that lucky corner. The rest of the country could wallow in pessimism if it chose but Hollywood was blatantly optimistic. Hollywood in general and Warner Brothers in particular dealt in dreams. Whether those dreams would ever come true really didn't matter. The dreams made money. The Kansas City farmer and the lobster fisherman in Maine needed a dream to cope with a rough reality and musicals defined the elusive dream better than anything else in the decade of the Depression.

But the Warren and Dubin phenomenon had not yet occurred and Al was still working with Burke.

Burke and Dubin wrote a song not used in any of the movies, called "For You," which made the Hit Parade in December 1948—almost four years after Al's death.

> *I will gather stars out of the blue*
> *for you, for you.*
> *I'll make a string of pearls out of the dew,*
> *for you, for you.*
> *Over the highway and over the street*
> *Carpets of clover I'll lay at your feet.*
> *Oh, there's nothing in this world I wouldn't do—*
> *For you, For you.*

Another big hit for the Burke-Dubin team was "Dancing with Tears in My Eyes," which Al claims to have gotten the inspiration for while enjoying a night on the town at the Coconut Grove. He spotted many young women dancing with men old enough to be their fathers and began speculating if they could really love these older men or were they with them only because the men could afford to support them or give them "goodies" they could not afford on Depression wages. But surely, schemed Al, there was a young man in the background who really was the one she wanted.

> For I'm dancing with tears in my eyes
> Cause the boy in my arms isn't you.
> Dancing with somebody new
> When it's you that my heart's calling to!
> Trying to smile once in a while
> But I find it so hard to do!
> For I'm dancing with tears in my eyes
> Cause the boy in my arms isn't you!

Though Al loved what he was doing, he began to resent the constant demands of the studio and the lack of appreciation from his superiors. Being an extremely sensitive man, unable to take criticism of any kind, he cringed after pouring heart, soul and expertise into a lyric only to have someone crumple it up, toss it in the wastepaper basket, saying, "Try again. It's lousy."

Though Al tried hard to find satisfaction in his family, the move to Southern California did little for his rocky relationship with his wife. Helen missed the climate and hustle-bustle of New York City; the faster-paced lifestyle. What we would now call the laid-back ways of Hollywood did not appeal to her. Finally, she

didn't like the so-called "Hollywood crowd," made up of Al's friends and colleagues. Again it was a stand-off between the songwriter and his lady.

But Al came up with a solution. He led a double life, masquerading as a family man at appropriate times and pursuing the hedonistic life at other times. He stepped in and out of the roles at will, drinking heavily, developing frequent attacks of anxiety, more and more needful of his hideaway spots. Women drifted in and out of his life.

When Al Dubin was playing the role of family man, life was good for me and my sister. There were trips to San Francisco, glorious days at Santa Anita watching the races in the golden, thin winter sun that is so special in December in Southern California. There were long, leisurely rides in that pre-freeway era south to old Del Mar and the race track in which Al held stock. His box seat was next to Bing Crosby's and my sister and I had a hard time keeping our minds on the horses with such a celebrated star so close to us. It was a happy time for Bing, too. His first wife Dixie Lee was expecting twins.

One of my earliest memories is of the old race track at Tijuana when we had first landed in Southern California and I was about six years old. I had not mastered the skill of reading so my father patiently read the program to me and I selected a 60-1 shot called "Dolly Bay." Al put $2.00 for me on Dolly Bay and, on a hunch, put a $100 bet for himself. When the horse won, he got even for the day, paid the hotel bill, bought my mother a present and presented me with a shiny silver dollar.

In addition to learning a lot about gambling, I learned to read in Tijuana by poring over the programs

and trying to comprehend the intricacies of the Racing Form. I learned to recognize such names as George Wolfe and Ralph Neeves before I mastered "Jump, Spot, Jump."

My father would explain to me which of the jockies drank and told me never to bet on them in the later races as they would be too smashed to give their horses a good ride.

Though he had access to "hot tips," he still managed to leave the track most of the time minus thousands of dollars.

About this time, Warner Brothers let Joe Burke go and, though Al feared he might be the next to feel the axe, he decided to stay on in Hollywood. He told Joe that he thought he could get a job writing scenarios if the musical boom should boomerang.

Joe and Al corresponded frequently and in one letter Joe told Al that his son James, a student at Villanova, complained that the school did not have a decent Alma Mater. Would Al be interested in writing a lyric if he, Joe, composed a tune? Al sat down and immediately answered "yes." The song is still being sung by current Villanova students.

Al loved this sort of lyric-writing. It was his passport to immortality. He did not envision people singing "Forty-Second Street" for years and years to come, but he knew that a school song or a Navy or Marine hymn would go on almost forever. And so a little bit of Alexander Dubin would never be forgotten. Such a thought thrilled the man.

During this period, Al wrote a song called "Crosby, Columbo and Vallee," recognizing the enormous popularity of these three men with the public. The

songwriter respected talented singers and was much saddened by Russ Columbo's untimely death. Al and Columbo had written a song together, "Only a Voice on the Air," shortly before Columbo died.

There was a song making the rounds with an off-beat minor key melody. Al put lyrics to the tune, calling it "Too Many Tears" and also authored lyrics for "Three's a Crowd" which was used in a musical called *Crooner.* The composer of both songs was Harry Warren.

Harry had come to orange-tree land as a "package deal" from a publishing firm, just as Al Dubin had. And just as Al had fallen in love with the place, Harry hated it. He missed New York and was often on the verge of packing up and returning to Forest Hills.

But, of course, Harry had a date with destiny and with Al Dubin. It was time for the start of a collaboration that was to prove one of the most phenomenally successful of Hollywood musical partnerships. It was 1932, the year Franklin Delano Roosevelt was elected and the year Warner Brothers produced *Forty-Second Street.*

Al and Harry wrote four songs for *Forty-Second Street*—the title song, "Shuffle Off to Buffalo," "Young and Healthy," and "You're Getting to Be a Habit with Me." Remarkably, all four of the songs were hits. Al and Harry also had a bit part in the movie, which starred Ruby Keeler, Dick Powell, Warner Baxter, George Brent and Bebe Daniels. They played themselves, songwriters for a musical, and Al got a kick out of seeing himself on the screen even though he looked more like a thug than an affable songwriter.

Al made friends with other talents at Warner Brothers—Busby Berkeley, Ray Heindorf, Leo

Forbstein, Lloyd Bacon. Heindorf and Forbstein were talented musicians who arranged, scored, conducted the musicians and translated Harry's melodies from lead sheet to film. Lloyd Bacon was a director.

Helen bought a new gown to wear to the premiere of *Forty-Second Street* which was held at Grauman's Chinese Theater on Hollywood Boulevard. I rehearsed for a week in my bathroom mirror, just in case a photographer might want a picture of a skinny nine-year-old with straight hair and buck teeth. Not only did I not have to fight off the photographers, but neither did my father. In 1932, songwriters had no celebrity status with either the public or the studios for whom they worked. However, Jack Warner knew a good thing when he saw it and *Forty-Second Street* was a smashing success with critics and at the box office. In fact, it was voted one of the top ten films of 1933. (Though it was made in 1932, it was not released until 1933.) Warner duly noted that the picture boasted four songs that translated into four hits. The track record—four for four—couldn't get much better than that!

Though Harry had returned to New York after completing *Forty-Second Street,* he hurried back to Lotus Land when Jack Warner offered him and Al Dubin a yearly renewable contract at higher salary. Though Harry was reluctant, Al was jubilant. He wanted to live in California where he was close to the border towns of Tijuana and Juarez, to the gambling spots and the brothels. He wanted to be close to San Francisco where they served such tasty crab and shrimp on Fisherman's Wharf and where he could enjoy a meal at John's Rendezvous—his favorite San Francisco eatery. Why, he could be in the desert in a couple of hours and in

snow-covered mountains a couple of hours after that. As far as Al was concerned, California had it all.

The songwriters were assigned to come up with a score for *Gold-Diggers of 1933*. The plot of that musical was that of a show within a show, but actual production numbers were often determined by Dubin's lyrics. Songs were "I've Got to Sing a Torch Song," "Shadow Waltz," "Remember My Forgotten Man," "We're in the Money" and "Pettin' in the Park."

"Remember My Forgotten Man" was a unique song for its day. Actually, it was a song of social protest, a genre which, though familiar to every child of the sixties, was unheard of in the era of the "tune-moon-June-spoon" era of the thirties.

> *Remember my forgotten man;*
> *You put a rifle in his hand—*
> *You sent him far away,*
> *You shouted "Hip, Hooray!"*
> *But look at him today.**

In fact, a few years later, the song still being popular, the censors refused to allow the song to be performed via the air-waves, contending that the lyrics were not in the best interests of the country's morale and were "subversive." Al loved that; he took it as a real compliment and it promptly became one of his favorite lyrics.

For though Al was then living high off the hog, he was painfully aware of the suffering of the vast numbers of unemployed, often explaining that his way of helping out was to write songs that everyone could sing to help

---

*"Remember My Forgotten Man." Lyric by Al Dubin, music by Harry Warren. © 1933 (renewed) Warner Bros. Inc. All rights reserved. Used by permission.

them forget about all those things they didn't have—like rent money. Neither did he ever forget it was the "little guy" and the "little gal" (financially speaking) who sang his songs, bought his songs and enabled him to live the elegant lifestyle. He respected his "customers," unlike many Hollywood personalities of the day who exploited and laughed at a public so gullible, so hungry for dreams. Al couldn't laugh at them because he was just as dream hungry as they were.

He often entertained the fantasy that he was a humble bank clerk, going faithfully to work each morning and returning to the "little woman" each night for a rich romantic life.

> *For I'm the boy whose only joy is loving you—*
> *Who worries till he hurries home when day is through—*
> *And I'm the guy you give your good-night kisses to—*
> *Remember me?**

Al Dubin had a talent for putting his lyrical finger on the moment. "We're in the Money" was just what people wanted to hear in 1933—money was on everyone's mind—*"Let's lend it, spend it, send it rolling along."*** Everybody felt like that in 1933 and Al condensed those feelings in a few words.

Just as he was impressed with the disaster of the Depression, Al had been impressed when Irving Berlin married the wealthy socialite Ellin Mackay in 1925, and

*"Remember Me?" Lyric by Al Dubin, music by Harry Warren. © 1937 (renewed) Warner Bros. Inc. All rights reserved. Used by permission.
**We're in the Money." Lyric by Al Dubin, music by Harry Warren. © 1933 (renewed) Warner Bros. Inc. All rights reserved. Used by permission.

he and Jimmy McHugh had written "When a Kid Who Came from the East Side Found a Sweet Society Rose."

Al was able to put into words what the majority felt, so people who sang his songs often had that feeling of recognition—"Ah, yes, that's the way it is." And therein lay the secret, in part, of Al Dubin's success. Certainly there were cleverer, more sophisticated lyricists. But Al, terribly schmaltzy at times, seemed to be able to speak for people's vulnerable feelings—nothing profound, just the way someone would feel at the end of a love affair.

> *I've got to sing a torch song*
> *For that's the way I feel.*
> *When I feel a thing*
> *Then I can sing,*
> *It must be real.*
>
> *I couldn't sing a gay song.*
> *It wouldn't be sincere.*
> *I could never croon a happy tune*
> *Without a tear.**

Gold Diggers of 1933 over, *Footlight Parade* was in the wings, waiting for new lyrics. Things began to get tough for Al. Pressure was building. He travelled back to New York City frequently. He moved in and out of the house he happened to be living in at the time. One month he would be esconced in a Malibu home, the next he would rent a house in the Valley, an apartment in Hollywood.

He began to disappear from the scene.

Everyone who knew Al had a story to tell about his disappearing acts. Some of the outrageous stories are

*"I've Got to Sing a Torch Song." Lyric by Al Dubin, music by Harry Warren. © 1933 (renewed) Warner Bros. Inc. All rights reserved. Used by permission.

true—others, like many stories about the man's capacity for food and drink, are apocryphal.

Early in his life, Al had learned to retreat to his bedroom when his parents quarreled or lectured him concerning the future joys of medical school. He didn't argue. He ran from problem-solving. The trait grew as he grew; only the avenues of escape grew increasingly dangerous.

As he had disappeared from New York to hole up at Dad's Hotel in Philadelphia, he had to disappear from time to time from his family, his friends and Warner Brothers, giving ulcers to those he worked with and migraines to the men who paid his salary. Al could never understand why everyone got so upset when he vanished. After all, he was working while he drank in the Stud Saloon in Tijuana, rested at the Taft Hotel in New York or fulfilled certain needs at a bawdy house in Juarez. Just because most lyricists chose to work in a stuffy office from approximately nine to five didn't mean that the rule applied to him. He felt that if he produced—and produce he did!—then nothing else mattered. It was the same logic he propounded at Perkiomen School—if he could win honors for the school in track, football, basketball, writing their songs, did it really matter if he showed up for chemistry class? Al didn't think so. He was an elitist with his own set of rules.

Art Schwartz, a good friend to Al and an employee of Warner Brothers, was frequently elected to bring Al back to the lot to finish the current musical. On one occasion, Art found Al in Dinty Moore's, one of his favorite eateries in New York.

"You know we have to catch that Super Chief back to California, Al. They're waiting for you."

"Just let me order another pastrami sandwich and I'll go with you."

"Don't you want to pack?" Art asked Al.

"No, I'll just leave everything for the maid. She was awfully nice. Let's go right to the station and we can be on the coast by Saturday," Al said.

Art was delighted. It had been easy this time.

Jovial, affable Al boarded the train with nothing but some badly crumpled lead sheets in his back pocket and a couple of bottles of rye whiskey. He set about drinking the rye whiskey in the compartment he and Art shared and tried to work on the lyrics.

It was not coming off the way he wanted. That certain word or phrase he needed was not there. Though inside Al panicked, Art knew nothing of it—all he could see was this fat man drinking whiskey and writing a lyric.

The train pulled into the Albuquerque, New Mexico, station.

"I need to stretch my legs and I want to buy Helen and the girls some jewelry or blankets," Al told his friend.

"Sure, Al, that's a good idea."

Art felt it was a good idea because the bottle of whiskey was about empty and he thought the fresh air would be good for Al. Art dozed a minute and awoke to the call of "All aboard!" Al hadn't returned to the compartment. Al wasn't in the club car or the toilet. Al Dubin had not gotten back on the train.

Two weeks later, Al showed up at the studio, lyrics completed and acceptable.

Art approached him and said, "Al, you let me down. You promised we would be on the coast by Saturday. Remember?"

"Sure, Art," Al replied, putting an arm around his small friend's shoulder. "Sure, Arty, but I didn't say which Saturday."

He didn't always take the Super Chief to New York when he felt the need to get away. Havana was one of his favorite "forget-the-real-world" spots. There were bawdy houses, exotic food and drink and gambling there. What more could a man want?

When he disappeared to Rosarita Beach in Baja California, he would disappear in style in his pink custom Cord, driven by William Moore, his black chauffeur who was almost as much a legend at the studio as his employer.

At three a.m. William was often awakened with "Let's go to Mexico." It could have been Tijuana, Juarez, Rosarita Beach or Ensenada, depending on Al's mood of the moment.

Harry Warren got a call from Al one night in 1935. They were working on a musical titled *Stars Over Broadway* when Al disappeared. They had already written more than twenty songs that year for musicals that included "Go into Your Dance," "Gold Diggers of 1935," "Broadway Gondolier," "Page Miss Glory," "Shipmates Forever," "Sweet Music," "Living on Velvet" and "In Caliente."

Harry was worried about his partner Al because he could see the pressure building for the fat man. It was building for him, too, and, worse, there was no respite in sight. They were to write the score for two more mu-

sicals and contribute songs to at least three other pictures before the year was out.

A call for Harry came at two a.m.

"Hi, Harry. How's everything?" asked Al.

"Al, where the hell are you?" asked Harry.

"Listen, Harry, I'm in Juarez, but listen," he said, excited now, "I have a lyric. But listen, I just ate some quail
and they were delicious."

"Al, are you in a restaurant?"

"No, I'm at the local cat house. I got my inspiration
right here, Harry. I just finished the lyrics for that great
tune of yours." And with that, Al sang Harry the lyrics
of "Where Am I, Am I in Heaven?"

Mexico and Cuba were private hideaways, and sometimes New York fit that category. San Francisco, Palm
Springs, Arrowhead Springs, Lake Arrowhead, Catalina, Del Mar, La Jolla were family hideaways.

Those family trips were special times for me, whether
they were spent dunking shrimp in hot sauce on San
Francisco's Fisherman's Wharf, browsing through a
bookstore, trotting by my father's side in Chinatown to
be treated to dinner in some dark, mysterious restaurant, swimming in the Cove in La Jolla, visiting the
Chicago World's Fair.

Al Dubin, with his special quality, could transform
Tijuana into Granada, the Del Mar Race Track into the
Roman chariot races. He had a gift of magic—of letting
others see a beauty, a glamor that was not there before
they experienced it with him.

Jo Warren, Harry's wife, attended the 1932 Olympics
in Los Angeles with Al and felt like a queen as he
granted her every wish. "You want a hot dog?" He
would buy the whole tray of hot dogs. "Want a souve-

nir? Let's have six of them—in case they get lost or turn out to be valuable in the years ahead." Not that Al Dubin gave much thought to the years ahead. He lived always in the "now."

Harry didn't spend enough time with his pretty wife, Al thought. So he convinced Harry to take Jo to Tijuana for the races and the Jai Lai games. A new world opened up for Jo as she was allowed to join in the pleasures usually reserved for the men folk.

"I loved travelling to New York on the Super Chief with Al and Harry. Al always had a private compartment and lots of drinks on hand—and whatever delicacies the Super Chief had to offer. I always felt special when I was with him. He opened up whole new worlds for me and I was always sorry for him that his wife didn't share some of these special times with him."

Yes, Al Dubin travelled in style, ate with style, wrote with style and endowed all his relationships with style—Helen Dubin excepted.

While other songwriters were cultivating friends among the bandleaders who would play and "plug" their songs, Al was greatly teased because his closest friend among the bandleaders was Harry Owens who played nothing but Hawaiian music and who often wrote his own songs.

The bandleader speaks with great affection of Al Dubin in his book *Sweet Leilani*. When the Musicians' Union went on strike at the Beverly Wilshire Hotel, Al Dubin was chosen to give Owens the news about the impending strike which would put all of his musicians out of work. Al softened the blow in his unique fashion by ordering champagne and caviar sent to a suite at the Beverly Wilshire where he was staying for a few days

while his latest house in the Valley was being readied for rental. Owens, very upset by the loss of his job, was lying on his bed, dejectedly, when his phone rang. It was Al, inviting him to come up to his suite. "No good to be alone on a night like this," said Al.

At the Biltmore Bowl in 1937, where the Academy Awards were held, Harry Owens won the coveted award for best song for "Sweet Leilani."

"The nice guy," writes Owens, "was genuinely happy for me, happier, if possible, than if *he* had won the Oscar."

Al embraced Harry at the Biltmore Bowl and congratulated him warmly but it took an awful lot of rye whiskey on the rocks to drown his disappointment. His own nominated song, "Remember Me?" had not made it. He wanted so badly the thrill of beating the Gershwins, George and Ira, whose song "You Can't Take That Away from Me" was also nominated.

Al Dubin felt that if one of his songs failed, then he was a failure. He could not separate himself from his lyrics. His self-worth depended on each song being a hit—an impossible goal to set for oneself. He was still telling long-dead Simon Dubin that, "Yes, he could write songs for a living. He could be a success." And though he was able to live well with the money he earned, he still panicked each time he was assigned to write a lyric and was plunged into despair if each song did not make the Hit Parade.

Though he did not feel important himself, often mocking what skill he possessed as a lyricist, he had the unique ability of making others feel important. No small talent, that. It was a quality I truly appreciated as a child. While other adults in my world always seemed in

a hurry to get away and get on with the business of grownup living, my father acted as if watching me catch the brass ring on the old Santa Monica Pier carousel was the most enjoyable project he had ever undertaken. He acted as if a game of Old Maid played on the big white steamer that sailed to Catalina was every bit as important as a new lyric.

Together, my father and I rode the roller boats at Venice Pier, conquering danger each time we made a successul "landing"; walked the sands at Malibu; hiked trails in the mountains; fed the animals at San Francisco's Fleischacker Zoo. We stuffed on breakfast at Musso Frank's; ate greasy hot dogs smeared with yellow mustard at the Pier; played Bingo in Venice.

His bosses worried about Al; Harry Warren suffered some feelings of apprehension from time to time. But I thought my father was the only person in this world who could do no wrong. And he loved the pure unadulterated adoration only a little girl could give.

Al Dubin knew how to treat a lady, be she seven or seventy.

THERE IS A PUBLICITY STILL photo taken of Al when he was under contract to Warner Brothers which shows him sitting in front of a table laden with food, knife and fork in hand, ready to begin the fugue of the fat man. He had a reputation as a gigantic overeater and the reputation was deserved though some of the stories about his love of food are apocryphal.

One story has it that he would fly to New Orleans on impulse just to dine at Antoine's. Not true. Al Dubin was never on a plane in his life. He was terrified of them. Other stories call him a gourmet. Not true. He didn't have a discriminating palate but opted for quantity over quality.

When Helen and Al had been married only a short time, she invited his brother Joe, another overeater, to their New York apartment for breakfast. Between them, Joe and Al ate two dozen eggs, two pounds of bacon, one dozen ears of corn and four of five pounds of pickled pigs' feet. She didn't remember if they ate des-

sert but they did eat a loaf or two of toasted corn rye with the bacon and eggs.

Lindy's, Sardi's, Dinty Moore's and Longchamps were his favorite eating places in New York City while his haunts in Los Angeles included Armstrong Schroeders in Beverly Hills, the Vine Street and Beverly Hills Brown Derby, Eaton's Chicken House, Musso Frank's and supper clubs of yesterday on the Sunset strip—the Clover Club, where he could gamble, Ciro's and Mocambo and a small restaurant on Sunset and La Brea called Gene's where the Southern cook prepared chicken so meltingly delicious that Al even ate the bones.

Al was dining with friends late one night at Armstrong Schroeders. He had eaten the steak dinner, with all the trimmings, and was enjoying his after-dinner drink and cigar when a latecomer arrived and ordered lobster. Al thought it looked delicious and called the waitress over to order a complete dinner for himself

"But, Al," his friend reminded him. "You just finished. Even you must be full. Where are you gonna put the food?"

Al went to the men's room, stuck his finger down his throat, came back and polished off the lobster. The friend who had followed him to the men's room was appalled. Al didn't want to miss any of life's pleasures. It was all here to be enjoyed, to be tasted, drunk, savored, loved.

When the songwriter entered a restaurant, he expected service immediately. Because he was a big tipper, he usually got it. But finding out through experience that he could not always get the waiter's attention at a

crowded nightclub where he frequently took several friends, he had a system. He ordered four or five drinks for everybody as soon as the waiter appeared. The waiter was surprised but Al persisted.

"This way," he cheerfully explained, "we won't have to be at the mercy of some busy waiter. And by the time these run out, we can probably catch his eye."

Just as there were his hideaway vacation spots and his family vacation spots, Al had two sets of restaurants. There were the ones where he went with his family and the ones where he went with friends, colleagues and/or mistresses. He usually insisted that his wife pick the Sunday night restaurant but seldom liked her selection, calling them "Helen's tearooms."

Helen ate sparingly, didn't drink hard liquor, wine or beer, and enjoyed simple fare. Clearly, they could not find a restaurant to fill both their needs. But my father handled the problem well. When all four of us would go to a "tearoom"-type restaurant, he would order one of the more filling entrees and when the waitress returned to ask: "Will there be anything else?" he would reply, "Yes. Just do this," indicating his empty plate, "all over again."

My sister Marie was terribly embarrassed by his gluttony but I was so young the first time he did it that I just thought everybody's father acted like that.

More than once I shared cold baked beans, eaten out of the can, with my father by a stream or in a park and he savored the beans with the same relish that he savored delicate shad roe served to him in an expensive restaurant. He liked the food, not the ambience.

All of this food, eaten consistently, not just on special occasions, resulted in a severe case of obesity. He was

five feet, nine inches tall and he weighed at his heaviest over 300 pounds.

But Al was an incurable romantic and in fantasy saw himself as the slender, personable youth of Perkiomen days, muscles taut from track and football, body healthy and slim with food selected from the training table.

But fantasy flew out the window when Al confronted his enormous body in the mirror. He was fat! The excess weight aggravated severe varicose veins, contributed to a couple of minor heart attacks. Though he bought specially tailored suits from Hollywood tailors Mariani-Davis and wore monogrammed silk underwear to compensate for a body misshapen by fat and neglect, he suffered agony over his obesity—agony he refused to share with others.

He admitted his hatred of his fat body one day to his wife when he tried to run 100 yards, his specialty in prep school days. He could not run 50 yards and stood in the street, alternately panting, retching and crying. "I am old! I'm an old man! I can't run anymore." He was just thirty-nine. His reasoning was pessimistically faulty; he could not stop the years, yet he would do nothing about his weight. He never even entertained the idea of a diet and went without food only during drinking bouts.

He handled his pain and disgust by joking about his obesity and successfully convinced friends and colleagues that he was a fat, jovial man to whom eating took precedence over personal pride.

The jokes were corny and trite.

"I have T.B., Patti,"

"You do, Daddy?" I would ask, playing straightman for him.

"Yeah, T.B.—two bellies."

"You know where I have my suits made, Patti?"

"No, Daddy, where do you have your suits made?"

"I have my suits made at Omar the Tentmakers."

His stomach, at one point, was so huge that he complained to his wife that he could not wash his feet, so when she remodeled their home, she put a seat in his shower. That was good for many more jokes on himself at Hollywood parties.

Everything was a joke to Al. At least that is what he pretended to others in order to hide his extreme sensitiveness. He joked about his Jewishness and knew every anti-Semitic joke going the rounds. It was all right if he told them or if he poked fun at a "stereotype" characteristic, but he would not tolerate the same behavior from Gentiles.

In serious moments, he earnestly discussed Jewish history, mourning for the Jew, deprived of land and forbidden to support himself by farming. He combined anger and sadness in his voice when he talked about the pogroms in Poland and Russia where Al's ancestors had lived.

Though there was little discrimination among studio personnel—writers, directors, producers, actors, other songwriters—there was moderate to severe discrimination in other areas of Al's life.

His reaction to the New York City apartment signs of "No dogs; no Jews" was one of bitterness, but a bitterness he buried, or tried to drown with liquor or turned into a joke on himself. Confrontation of the problem was not his way. Though he sometimes acted as if the discrimination had gotten to him and he was in danger

of becoming an anti-Semite himself, he was, in reality, fiercely proud of his heritage. He just couldn't fight for it.

He joined the Del Mar Beach Club in the thirties. Most of the beach clubs, including the Bel Air Bay Club and the Jonathan Club observed a policy of not admitting Jews or "picture people." The Del Mar Club advertised no such restrictions so Al felt doubly betrayed when the manager of the club said, "Our members are among the finest. We have several celebrities like yourself and you won't be bothered by common riff-raff or Jews."

Al quietly told the manager he was a Jew and would the manager be good enough to return his initiation fee.

The red-faced manager apologized with the classic "You don't *seem* like a Jew" remark, pleading with him to stay on as a member. Because Al had joined primarily for the family—my sister and I loved to swim there with our friends—he overlooked the attack on his roots. But he paid a price in lowered self-esteem. The lower his self-esteem, the more he drank, the more he ran to his hideaways.

When Al was living with the family, he and Helen rented a large Spanish house on Mansfield Drive in Los Angeles. My sister and I loved the old two-story place because we each got our own bedroom. The realtor who rented him the house was a delightful Italian lady. She was enchanted with Al Dubin and glad to have a Hollywood "picture person" rent the house and become her neighbor at the same time.

"I am so glad you rented the house, Mr. Dubin. You know, it could have been some Jew."

"Perhaps you should rent the house to someone else, You see. I am a Jew."

Again the "Oh, Mr. Dubin, you aren't like those other Jews. And you are so talented." (Al often wondered what those "other Jews" were really like!)

He deferred to his wife and to me and my sister. We liked the house—after all, my mother and sister were Gentiles. He would swallow his rage once again, cope with his pain with the bottle.

Sometimes another's anti-Semitism genuinely amused him. Harry and Al's office was being renovated and the hammering proved nerve-shattering to Harry, who was trying to compose. Now Harry Warren barked like an anti-Semite but he just never lived like one.

"I can't work here," Harry declared angrily, leaving the piano to take off for the commissary, glowering at the workman as if it were all his fault.

The workman turned to Al and in a conspirational tone said, "These damn Jews are all alike. They think they own the world. Who does that little kike think he is anyway?"

Al couldn't move his 300-pound frame fast enough to get to the commissary and report the incident to Harry, relishing every word. Harry snarled at Al and then the two of them started to laugh and Al told him: "You should be awfully glad, Harry, that I accept Jews!"

The only person Al really communicated with concerning the pain he felt at others' anti-Semitism was his younger brother Joe. Joe was making a name for himself as an arranger and a composer for both Universal Studios and Walt Disney Studios. Al was simultaneously very proud of Joe and slightly jealous. He envied Joe's

Al Dubin. This is one of the last photographs taken of him, probably in the early forties.

Perkiomen Seminary's star athlete. At left, captain of the football team. Above, seated at far right, star of the track team. Below, on the left at top of the stairs, all 'round ball player.

Publicity shot of Helen McClay, of Kitner, Hawksley and McClay, circa 1916.

Harry Warren and Al Dubin, the most successful songwriting team
of the Golden Age of the Hollywood Musical.

Al and Harry posing with actor Hugh Herbert.

Al took readily to California and dressed accordingly. Here he poses happily with stepdaughter Marie, daughter Patricia, and wife Helen.

Al and Helen in 1934, at the height of his success. An afternoon at the track seems in the offing.

happy marriage at the same time he made jokes about Joe's wife Ethel.

One story Al loved to tell (apocryphal or not) was of leaving a San Francisco restaurant with Joe and Ethel Dubin when a young woman approached them selling gardenias from a tray.

"No, thank you," said Ethel, "we've eaten already."

Ethel Dubin did not like her brother-in-law, not because he made fun of her—but because she felt he was a bad influence on her husband. Joe started losing money at Santa Anita race track and Ethel told Al that Joe only gambled to imitate his brother. So Al decided to speak to Joe about this.

"Joe, you shouldn't be going to the track and losing all that money. Ethel doesn't like it."

"But, Al, you do it all the time," Joe replied in surprise at the admonition.

"Joe, do as I say, not as I do."

The same thing occurred when I began to play the slot machines around the age of eleven. Al was furious when my allowance would disappear in a day. When I explained—quite logically, I thought—that he had, indeed, taught me how to gamble at a very tender age, he lost his temper. He never could see the connection between his actions and those who loved and admired him trying to behave as he did. Again—"Do as I say; not as I do."

Ethel Dubin also blamed Joe's drinking on Al. Joe was just trying to behave like his brother and soon gave it up of his own accord.

Joe and Al had a strange relationship. They cared about each other but they were wary, one of the other.

Al was fiercely proud of Joe's considerable talent and at the same time terrified that Joe might make a bigger name for himself than he had. He proudly told his friends that Joe was the only person in the world who could beat him at anagrams but he was annoyed every time it happened and finally stopped challenging Joe to a game.

Al Dubin could be proud of you, impressed with you—but just don't surpass him. That was too hard for him to take, especially from a brother.

EIGHT

JAMES CAGNEY was dressed in a sailor suit. The "girl-next-door," wholesome good looks still shone through the exotic Chinese pajama costume of Ruby Keeler. Jimmy and Ruby danced and danced and danced and Cagney sang the lyrics to "Shanghai Lil."

> *I've covered every little highway*
> *And I've been climbing every hill.*
> *I've been lookin' high and I've been lookin' low—*
> *Lookin' for my Shanghai Lil.*
>
> *The stars that hang high over Shanghai*
> *Bring back the memory of a thrill, etc.**

The musical was called *Footlight Parade*. "The Madman," Dubin and Warren's nickname for Busby Berkeley, was stumped for an idea for a lavish and dif-

*"Shanghai Lil." Lyric by Al Dubin, music by Harry Warren. © 1933 (renewed) Warner Bros. Inc. All rights reserved. Used by permission.

131

ferent number. Dubin offered it to him with the "Shanghai Lil" lyric. Everybody loved it. And with Cagney and Keeler to perform it, how could it miss?

The next project was *Roman Scandals,* a Samuel Goldwyn film, starring Eddie Cantor. Al was in New York in 1933 on a family vacation and Harry was there visiting relatives. They all got together with Cantor in a local hotel suite and Harry claimed that Al came up with the idea for the musical to be set in ancient Roman days, complete with gorgeous, half-naked slave girls. What possibilities!

Al and Harry wrote five songs for *Roman Scandals*— "Keep Young and Beautiful," "Rome Wasn't Built in a Day," "No More Love," a torchy ballad sung hauntingly by Ruth Etting, "Put a Tax on Love" and "Build a Little Home."

Berkeley was daring and innovative with the "No More Love" production number. There were a dozen beautiful girls, covered only by body stockings but appearing naked to the viewer, their bodies artistically covered by long, blonde wigs. They sang and swayed erotically, hands and feet in chains.

It was controversial both at the studio and in the Dubin household.

Helen said, "Al, you are certainly not going to let Marie and Patti see that. I think it is disgusting—all those girls nude. Shocking!"

"It's artistic. There's nothing dirty about it at all. I don't see why the girls can't see it. It won't hurt them."

We saw it! We loved it!

It was about this time that the Hays Office and the Legion of Decency came upon the Hollywood scene, making life difficult for movie producers. On Sunday morn-

ing at Good Shepherd Catholic Church in Beverly Hills, the priest from the pulpit asked us all to stand and repeat the Legion of Decency Pledge in which the person taking the pledge promised to avoid all "indecent and immoral motion pictures." My mother, of course, was reciting the pledge in a loud, clear voice when my father, still seated, pinched her hard on the arm, whispering, "Dammit! Sit down and shut up! Dirty movies are your bread and butter." Even Helen, torn by the dilemma between reality and religion, laughed about the incident later.

The next picture they worked on, *Moulin Rouge,* was also shot at the Goldwyn Studio though it was released by United Artists and produced by Darryl F. Zanuck. Dubin respected and admired Zanuck and enjoyed talking with him about their Eastern European ethnic roots. In many ways a sophisticated man, Dubin was naïve about a celebrity he really admired and felt just as starstruck by his association with Zanuck as any autograph-seeker felt at an opening night premiere in the presence of Dick Powell or Joan Blondell.

For *Moulin Rouge,* Al and Harry wrote "Boulevard of Broken Dreams," perhaps the theme song of Al's life, "Coffee in the Morning, Kisses at Night" and "Song of Surrender."

Goldwyn was mystified by Al, who did not write at the studio, didn't show up for pre-production meetings and was never around when his numbers were staged. He was forever asking Harry Warren, "Where's Dugan?" He never did discover that Al was a Jew.

In 1934, the songwriters wrote the scores for three more musicals. One of them, *Wonder Bar,* featured "Goin' to Heaven on a Mule." Al gave Berkeley the idea

for the pork chop tree used in the production number, and ate most of the pork chops! The sequence, elaborately staged, had been written as special material for Al Jolson who was identified with "black-face" numbers. Other songs were "Don't Say Goodnight," "Wonder Bar" and "Why Do I Dream Those Dreams?" The other two musicals of '34 were *Twenty Million Sweethearts* and *Dames*. *Dames* featured the title song of the same name, "The Girl at the Ironing Board," performed whimsically by Joan Blondell, and the song that was to become a standard—"I Only Have Eyes for You." *Twenty Million Sweethearts* gave forth "I'll String Along with You" and "Fair and Warmer."

Though life at the studio was hectic and Al was pressured, he was reaping the rewards of a job well done. Home life, on the contrary, brought no rewards. Money remained the biggest problem between Helen and Al—at least that is where the unhappy couple focused their grievances. Helen screamed, nagged and finally attached Al's salary. Nothing helped. So finally, on April 30, 1934, they separated formally (there had been many separations up to this point) and Al signed a property settlement wherein Helen was to receive 40 percent of his income, payments not to exceed $400 per week or fall below $150.

It was about this time that Harry Warren began asking Al, "How's the Irish cop?"—the Irish cop being Harry's nickname for Helen Dubin, who he always felt didn't understand his talented partner.

Al was fond of telling Harry that Helen wouldn't let him drink at home. She kept a very well-stocked bar and would not have minded if Al had a couple of drinks at cocktail time. But telling others he was not allowed to

drink booze in his own home had for Al a certain ring to it that was sure to garner sympathy for him. Al didn't really lie; he just didn't tell the whole truth.

Though Helen had been awarded the settlement and Al had signed the agreement, collecting the money was another matter. Often he did not have it, having lost it at the Clover Club, Tijuana, Santa Anita or in a poker game. Then he would hide out at someone's home if he was in town.

On one such occasion, Al stayed for five or six days at the home of songwriter Moe Jerome and his family. It was there that he finished the lyrics for "September in the Rain."

The Jeromes did not have a spittoon in the house, a real necessity if Al Dubin was your houseguest, so Al improvised one. Also Mrs. Jerome had just installed wall-to-wall carpeting. Stuart Jerome, their son, reports that his mother "was starting to get the vapors from thinking what would happen to her brand-new carpeting if he [Al] missed."

Continuing his remembrances of Al Dubin, Stuart Jerome said:

"As a kid, I found Al to be warm and kindly, especially with children. With adults, at least socially, I always had the feeling he was a little uncomfortable. He was close to being a genius, not only as a lyricist, but I think as a philosopher and poet. His brother Joe once confided that Al had written a thick looseleaf notebook of poems which Joe wanted to have published. Al refused any thought of publication, and later destroyed the notebook."

Not many people knew that Al Dubin spoke German well enough to translate or that he had studied Latin at

Perkiomen, or that he could sing a bit, or that he had been a first-rate athlete. Al seemed to enjoy playing the role of the ignorant, poorly educated, hard-drinking, vulgar slob who stained his office wall with tobacco juice.

I have heard that his language among men was flamboyantly colorful, but I never heard him swear and I never saw him drunk.

The ambivalent, contradictory side of this complex man was never more evident than in the money area. Lavishly generous to family and friends when he was in the mood, he would neglect to give his wife household money, sometimes for months at a time. He was not cruel or stingy, just irresponsible. If he lost $5,000 at the track, and he often did, well, it was his money, wasn't it? He felt that, having earned it, it was his to do with as he wished.

He would rationalize not giving Helen money in various ways.

"She nags too much."

"Helen can make one dollar do the job of ten and I know she has some put away for a rainy day and today it's raining!"

"Helen owns all the orange groves in Fullerton, so she doesn't need my money." (She never owned an orange tree, let alone an orange grove.)

Some people use money to make more money; to stash in the bank; to invest in business ventures; to buy stock, property, houses, apartments, boats. Al Dubin used money to buy pleasure, for himself and for others. He never planned ahead, never kept a record of checks written, never purchased property, never paid his income taxes. Al wanted money to jingle in his pocket. A

creature of impulse, he was delightfully spontaneous. A nurse who cared for him at a California hospital was given a horse just because she mentioned that she wanted one. He was often quick to grease an unknown palm while legitimate bills went unpaid. Like a child, he meant no harm; he just didn't understand budgets or balanced checkbooks, and he had no desire to learn.

Milton Cashy, a noted business manager for many Hollywood celebrities in the thirties, bravely took on Al as a client and, though he found him difficult to work with, became very fond of the man. By that time, the hostility between Helen and Al was open and fierce. Cashy took Al's side completely, disliking Helen's interference and her persistent insistence that Cashy put tighter controls on Al and send more money her way.

Like his hero, Edgar Allan Poe, Al gambled, drank to excess, incurred debts and made rhymes. No serious portrait of Al Dubin would be complete, no understanding of the man or comprehension of ideas for some of his lyrics would be possible, without mention of Edgar Allan Poe.

He discovered Poe either in his father's library at his boyhood home or at Perkiomen. But when he did, the discovery resulted in a lifelong devotion bordering on idolatry.

The rhythm and cadence of *The Raven* and *The Bells* fascinated Al and he loved to recite both, all the verses, to whomever would listen. *To Helen* was one of Al's favorites that he recited often to his wife. He was so taken with Poe's poem *Annabelle Lee* that he incorporated some of the lines in a song, published by Mills Music Co., that he entitled "Anne Lee." Dubin especially admired the alliteration in *The Bells* and his lyric for "Tip-

toe Through the Tulips with Me" were in reality an exercise in alliteration. He didn't dream that it would become a household phrase and that the 1929 song would be revived in the sixties, after his death.

Memories of this man reciting "The tintinnabulation of the bells, bells, bells" as he waved an unlighted, half-chewed cigar in the air still evoke from me a smile. Off would come his coat, up would go the shirt sleeves as his huge bulk darted about the room. Wide-eyed, feeling like I was being initiated into some sacred rites, I listened as he recited Poe.

Not only did Al admire the poetry and detective stories of Poe, he was fascinated by his life and strongly identified with him. He refused to accept the fact that Poe was a drug addict but thought of him more as a hapless alcoholic. Al contended that it was impossible to abuse alcohol and opium. The combination would kill.

The songwriter was fascinated by Poe's tender romance with his child bride and cousin, Virginia Clemm, who Poe called Annabelle Lee in his poetry.

Al also identified with Poe's unhappy life; his compulsive drinking; his heavy gambling; the fact that he was from Philadelphia; his love of the ladies; his rhyming; his impending sense of tragedy and doom; his fascination with the detective story.

Al's love of the detective story was an indiscriminate love. He could savor *The Murders in the Rue Morgue* one night and equally savor *True Detective Magazine* the next. When he discovered the delicacy of lobster, he didn't give up his fondness for ball-park franks.

Though Al saw Edgar Allan Poe as a tragic figure, he did not take himself seriously enough to dignify his own lifestyle with such a heavy adjective as "tragic." He

would have described his own life more as an ironic joke. The only thing Al took seriously in those days were his lyrics.

It's my opinion that my father's fascination with Poe's life influenced him, subliminally, in his eventual abuse of drugs. Rumor in Hollywood would have it that under extreme pressure from Warner Brothers' constant deadlines, Al started using pills to get going and to steady his nerves after a drinking bout. It is certainly a possibility, for during the decade of 1928 to 1938 Al Dubin wrote the words to over seventy hit film songs introduced in Warner Brothers musicals. Thirteen of the films boasted at least three hits from each score. How can you keep topping "Forty-Second Street," "I Only Have Eyes for You," "Lullaby of Broadway?" But that was what was expected of him and Harry Warren.

I do not know if he was using pills at this time, but he often called his doctor, Frederick Bergstrom, after heavy bouts of drinking.

It is difficult to understand how a man so sensitive, so unable to cope with ordinary problems of living, unable to balance a checkbook, shave himself or drive a car, could call up some mysterious inner resource to face the grind of the Golden Age of the Musical. But face it he did with a mind-boggling success ratio. To make things worse, Harry and Al were treated with very little respect or consideration during their association with Warner Brothers, where history was being made by both the good guys and the bad guys.

By 1935 many of the Tin Pan Alley gentlemen who had taken the train from East to West to seek fortune and fame with the "talkies" and the musicals had reversed their destinations—taking the Super Chief from

West Coast to East Coast. The studios found they had no need for such an influx of composers and lyricists.

But 1935 was the year of glory for Harry Warren and Al Dubin. They boasted eight songs on the Hit Parade and were presented with the Academy Award for their song "Lullaby of Broadway."

Other songs heard on "Your Hit Parade" that year, written by the now-famous team, were "She's a Latin from Manhattan," "About a Quarter to Nine," "Page Miss Gory," "The Rose in Her Hair," "Lulu's Back in Town," "Don't Give Up the Ship" and "Where Am I?"

Time magazine and *Colliers* published stories about the songwriting team. *Time* wrote of Harry's ulcers and Al's tobacco chewing and corn-cob pipe smoking. But though Dubin and Warren were beginning to be treated with respect by magazines, newspapers and the trade papers, Warner Brothers still had very little regard for either gentleman, but did agree to raise their salaries. Al was now getting $1,350 per week and Harry $1,500. Perhaps Warner Brothers felt topnotch lyricists were more easily replaceable than composers. At any rate, Al loved to tell people he didn't make as much money as Warren. It appealed to his offbeat sense of humor.

His offbeat sense of humor was never more evident than one night at a Sunset Strip restaurant. Accompanied by a very young starlet, Al turned to the man next to him at the dinner table and said, "I'm going to the men's room and I really don't mind if you fool around with my daughter while I'm gone." The rest of the men at the table, knowing Al, thought the incident

very funny, but the man he had spoken to was so appalled by the "degeneracy of the remark" that he left the party. Those Hollywood people!

In 1935 Al was living on the sand at Malibu in a rented house where his driver William Moore and William's wife, Nina, ran his household. He loved to go to sleep at night reading Poe and listening to the sound of the waves outside his front door.

One night he called Harry and said he had a surprise for him.

"I've written a song for you, Harry. I know how you still miss New York and this song is just for you. Come on down and I'll show it to you."

Harry drove to Malibu and Al played him "Lullaby of Broadway."

Jack Warner didn't like the lyric and wanted Al to write a new one. It was Harry who argued in favor of the lyric, claiming it went too well with the offbeat melody for another lyric to be written.

Harry and Al were loyal to one another, accepted each other's faults, foibles, eccentricities and peculiarites. Neither of them ever spoke a bad word about the other and, though they did not meet much socially, they stood tight together against the injustices and inequities of the studio and quickly learned to defend themselves as best they could. There was only one time Harry recalls that they had words with one another.

Harry had written a catchy melody for an Al Jolson movie in 1935, *Go Into Your Dance*. Al came back with a lyric but Harry said he didn't think the words went with the melody.

Al exploded! How dare Harry attack his strength? He knew, more than most lyricists, how to wed words to music.

"You know what the boys at the Brown Derby are saying about you, Harry? They're saying you've got a swelled head. That's what's wrong with you!"

And with that, Al did one of his disappearing acts to Mexico. When he returned, he had a new lyric for Harry's tune, "About a Quarter to Nine." He had also been relieved of hundreds of dollars in cash in a Nogales brothel.

Al had learned his lesson! But characteristically, he learned his lesson his way. He didn't give up Nogales and Mexicali and Rosarita Beach but he hired a private detective to protect him the next time he went there so that the same misfortune would not occur again.

Harry never judged Al's wild lifestyle but sympathized with him because he did not have a loving and understanding wife who, Harry felt, could have smoothed the rough edges for him.

When Marian Davies came to Warner Brothers, under the auspices of William Randolph Hearst, who was into making pictures, Al and Harry wrote the title song for *Page Miss Glory*. When the picture was over, Miss Davies tossed a lavish party for the entire crew and cast and remembered them all with gifts—all but the songwriters. It was easy to overlook songwriters, even in 1935 when the Hollywood musical was at its peak.

Harry and Al were exhausted as 1935 drew to a close, but their "Don't Give up the Ship" from the production *Shipmates Forever* was not only a Hit Parade selection but it was adopted by the Naval Academy as their service song, an honor that meant much to the sentimental side

of Al Dubin. He seldom bragged, adopting an attitude of humility at most times, but he made an exception in the case of "Don't Give Up the Ship."

In 1936, Dubin and Warren were to get very little rest after the exhausting previous year. They wrote songs for seven productions. "I'll Sing You a Thousand Love Songs" was one of the songs featured in *Cain and Mabel*, starring Marion Davies. Al Dubin was never happy with the lyric and was very surprised when it became first on the Hit Parade. *Gold Diggers of 1937*, produced in 1936, had another first on the Hit Parade, "With Plenty of Money and You." Other productions they wrote for were *Sing Me a Love Song, Hearts Divided, Colleen,* which was the last of the Ruby Keeler-Dick Powell musicals, *Sons o' Guns* and *Stolen Holiday.* The latter two featured no hit songs.

Early in 1936, Perkiomen School briefly re-entered Al Dubin's life in the form of a letter from Clarence Tobias, Headmaster, asking Al for a donation to the re- pair fund.

Al answered the request with the following letter.

Dear Mr. Tobias:

I am in receipt of your letter of the 18th and contents carefully noted.

Must refuse your request as well as contradict your statement that I have helped your school financially in the past, as I have not.

Perhaps you don't know that I was expelled one week before graduation and, though I may be prejudiced, I think unjustly.

For the past twenty years, your school has used my name in various publicity ballyhoo, as being a graduate of Perkiomen. You also to this day have used my "Alma Mater," which I wrote, and seen fit to drop my name

when printing it in your catalogue or on postcards, depriving me of credit for the authorship of same.

In view of the above facts, I think that my refusal of your request is consistent.

                                        Truly yours,

                                        Al Dubin

Several conciliatory letters later, Al agreed in August of 1936 to let them call on him for advice and help in arranging the Lloyd H. Schultz Memorial Fund, as "Red" Schultz had been a close friend of Al's during his Perkiomen days.

The Lloyd Schultz Memorial Chapel was dedicated at Pennsburg on October 10, 1936, but whether Al was too deep into a set of lyrics for Warners, had personal problems, or couldn't face former classmates, I don't know; he did not attend the service.

By 1937, Al Dubin was forty-six years old and very tired. He had given up his exciting Malibu house on the sand and was renting George Brent's estate in the Valley. He had the house, the pool, the servants, the girlfriends, the respect of his colleagues—and he was miserable.

He began to worry about his health and checked into the Mayo Clinic, leaving his Valley house in the capable hands of William and Nina Moore. Doctors at Mayo Clinic assured him that his heart was sound and they could find no evidence of what had been diagnosed as heart attacks in California. They did point out that he was abusing his body with excesses of food and whiskey.

He tried to forget his fears and decided to learn to drive a car when he returned to L.A. Al proudly drove the car for half a block and then asked my sister to go

and get it. The street, a quiet, residential one, was wide and deserted, but he was still too frightened to drive any farther. He couldn't sleep unless a light was left burning in or near his bedroom. He kept a gun in the glove compartment of his car. Increasingly, he unnerved his driver William by grabbing the wheel and screaming at imaginary roadblocks.

Helen Dubin recalled stories of his Perkiomen days when he had played all four quarters in a football game after he had been kicked in the head early in the game. She firmly believed a brain injury was responsible for some of his strange behavior.

But with all his problems, he contributed songs to five productions in 1937—*Mr. Dodd Takes the Air, The Singing Marines, Melody for Two, San Quentin* and *Marked Woman.* Five of the songs made the Hit Parade and two of them, "September in the Rain" and "Remember Me?" were number one on the popular radio show. "I Know Now," "'Cause My Baby Says It's So" and "How Could You?" were other Hit Parade choices in 1937.

Al was very proud of the fact that "The Song of the Marines" was adopted by the Marine Corps.

Though Al usually put his lyrics to Warren's melodies, "September in the Rain" was an exception. Al came up with the title, which he loved, and Harry wrote the melody around the title. But, during filming of *The Singing Marine,* Al disappeared and Johnny Mercer was called upon to finish the score.

Al was increasingly bothered that year by a fistula and engaged Dr. Vernon Hunt to perform the surgery. He spent his time recuperating at the Seventh Day Adventist Hospital in Loma Linda. He had William Moore pick him up nightly to take him for a hamburger or steak, as

he didn't take to the vegetarian menu served at the hospital.

The pain following his surgery was, in his words, "much worse than childbirth" and he was given a shot of morphine as needed to relieve the pain. When he left the hospital (he told his friends later) he took home with him a nurse who knew a doctor who asked few questions, and Al Dubin was well on his way to addiction. The woman had connections in New York and Al was eventually to travel there with her, meet the nurse's daughter, and embroil himself in his final tragedy of excesses and broken dreams. The nurse called herself Mrs. Perrin.

But Al managed to pull himself together to write "The Latin Quarter," "A Stranger in Paree," "Put That Down in Writing," "I Wanna Go Back to Bali" for *Gold Diggers in Paris.* It was the fifth edition of *Gold Diggers* that Al had worked on and he was bored with it. Since *Forty-Second Street,* Al had turned out eighty-eight songs which Warners had featured in twenty-eight pictures.

Johnny Mercer and Richard Whiting had been hired by Warner Brothers as a team, and when Whiting died Johnny did not have a composer to work with. Warners suggested that he work with Warren and collaborate on lyrics with Al Dubin.

Al felt, with his success record, that he didn't need a collaborator. Though he admired Mercer and correctly predicted he would be one of the great lyricists of all times, he understandably didn't want to collaborate with him though they did just that on "The Girl Friend of a Whirling Dervish." Al saw Johnny and Ginger Mercer socially and Johnny and Al became fast friends.

Another up-and-coming lyricist, Johnny Burke, was also one of Al's favorites and he considered him even

more talented, more "poetic" than Mercer. Al's favorite lyricist was Noel Coward and the lyric he admired the most was Coward's "Mad About the Boy." He considered Lorenz Hart the greatest of all the lyricists and thought Cole Porter was "overrated."

In reality, Dubin was jealous of the late, great, sophisticated, clever lyricist Porter. To add to that, Porter was a favorite of mine and the teenage crowd I hung out with in the thirties and Al found that difficult to take.

"I could have written nothing but sophisticated lyrics, too, if I had been a millionaire's son like Porter was. He wrote whatever he wanted to write. He could be innovative, creative. He wasn't writing songs for a living, but for a hobby. And Cole Porter didn't have to please Warner Brothers! I have to write lyrics that the general public will buy; songs that have commercial appeal; that make money. If I could have written whatever I wanted, whenever I wanted, I might have been a lot better lyric writer," he would say defensively.

He particularly disliked Cole Porter's "I've Got You Under My Skin" (which is one of the 100 most popular songs ever written) predicting it would never be a hit because it was a "phony" kind of title.

"When you say someone gets under your skin, it means they irritate you. It's not the right kind of title for a love song."

It was Al Dubin's only petulant remark in regard to other writers. He always gave lyricists their due and thought Mort Dixon, Irving Kahal and Mitchell Parish were deserving and underrated and would sing their praises just as convincingly as he sulked about the genius of Cole Porter.

IF DUBIN was petulant about Cole Porter's talent, he was outrightly furious at being forced to collaborate with the young Johnny Mercer on lyrics for *Garden of the Moon*. Dubin demanded that Warners buy out his contract even though his friend Harry Warren was exhorting him to stay. But Al wanted out; wanted to go back to New York to try to forget his humiliating experience of working with another lyricist. So Al, whose primary source of pleasure at this time was drugs, climbed aboard the Super Chief once again and settled down at the Taft Hotel in New York City.

Al didn't like to look at his life as he neared fifty. Disillusioned with his personal life, certain that his talent had not been appreciated by Warner Brothers, frightened that he might lose his ability to write, he sought solace more and more frequently in morphine.

With his reputation as a top Hollywood musical writer, Al had no trouble landing a job with the Olson and Johnson show, *Streets of Paris,* where he penned the

lyrics for his old friend, composer Jimmy McHugh. The Broadway musical included performers Bud Abbot and Lou Costello, Bobby Clark and the flamboyant South American singer Carmen Miranda. The show proved to be a hit, enjoying 274 performances in 1939. Songs included "South American Way," "Is It Possible?" and "Rendezvous Time in Paree."

Gladys Perrin lived with Al at the hotel during the week but went home to New Jersey by train every weekend. Al pressed her for details of where she went and what she did but she refused to tell the songwriter. When his curiosity grew to overwhelming proportions, Al hired a private detective who reported that a young, tall, beautiful blond girl in her teens met nurse Perrin at the train and they kissed and embraced affectionatelly. Al accused his nurse-lover of being a lesbian when she refused to tell him who the girl was. Finally, she admitted to him that the girl was her fifteen-year-old daughter who worked as a model. Al insisted on meeting her. Perrin postponed the meeting. Al pressed.

Finally, Edwina Coolidge entered Al Dubin's life. In his imagination, he must have become Edgar Allan Poe as he saw in the lovely Edwina the counterpart of Poe's child bride—Virginia Clemm. Virginia Clemm and Edwina Coolidge, or Edwina Perrin (she used both names), might have been close in age, but the resemblance stops there. This young woman was very sophisticated, coached by her mother on how to treat the songwriter.

Al often contended that he did not think Perrin was Edwina's mother because no mother would treat her daughter so cruelly, though he never cared to elaborate about the "cruel treatment" Edwina received.

At any rate, it was second-chance time for Al Dubin in the romance department. Fortified with morphine, led on by Edwina, he was briefly transported; he thought he had found the girl of his dreams.

He set up housekeeping with Edwina and her mother, determined to divorce Helen and marry his young girlfriend. He even wrote his wife, asking that I be allowed to come and live with them, but she refused. Al tried unsuccessfully to divorce Helen but the legal separation and the financial settlement with her proved binding and he was not free to marry.

While Edwina was pressing for marriage and a career in Hollywood, her mother was giving Al morphine injections on a fairly steady basis. But Al, so proficient in gratifying his desires instantly, couldn't or wouldn't see the disaster ahead. He was, he thought, in love.

If falling in love was significant in his personal life in 1939, one of the milestones of his professional life that year was publication of the Victor Herbert song "Indian Summer," which enjoyed the number one spot on "Your Hit Parade." The melody had been around for quite some time and Victor Herbert's daughter had invited songwriters to put lyrics to the unusual and beautiful tune. Many songwriters competed, among them Stanley Adams, former ASCAP president. But Al's lyric was selected and he was temporarily gratified by the honor. The song remained one of his favorite lyrics. That same year, he published "An Angel in a Furnished Room," which was written for the popular song market as opposed to a Hollywood musical or a Broadway show.

Al found it necessary to prove to himself, as well as to others, that he was versatile—that it wasn't just the

flashy Hollywood musical that he could write for or the Broadway show. He wanted to prove he could corner any market.

Stanley Adams says of Al Dubin, "[He] was the most versatile of the competent lyricists in our craft. He was a master of comedy, simplicity and sophistication, ballad, novelty and rhythm."

Composer Burton Lane says of him, "The quality of his lyrics was very high and, in my opinion, he ranks with the greatest lyric writers of our time."

The late Bing Crosby commented, "He had great talent as a lyric writer. I consider him certainly among the top five of all time."

Another Olson and Johnson production, *Keep Off the Grass,* was in the offing and Dubin and McHugh were rehired to compose the score. The show featured dancer Ray Bolger, Jimmy Durante and singer Virginia O'Brien. Songs included "Clear Out of This World," "A Latin Tune," "A Manhattan Moon and You," "I'm an Old Jitterbug" and "We're Here and Here Is Spring."

Lyrics from "Clear Out of This World" sadly seemed to reflect his drug experience of the time: *"I just feel a rosy glow. I don't seem to know where I am, where I go, what I do,"* or *"I'm all tangled and twirled into your beautiful scheme"* perhaps referred to Edwina.

In the song, "I'm an Old Jitterbug," Al says, *"I take my dancin' as a drug."* And sadly, wishfully thinking: *"On the floor I'm no slouch, I'm a killer on the couch."*

During this turbulent time, Al was in serious financial difficulty. All his money was going for drugs and to Gladys Perrin and Edwina. The once proud talent of the Hollywood musical was reduced to borrowing fives

and tens from the chorus girls in *Keep Off the Grass*. His habit was bigger than his pride.

Briefly, Al went to California in 1940 with Edwina and Gladys Perrin and wrote the lyrics for "Along the Santa Fe Trail," which appeared in the movie *The Santa Fe Trail*. It was during this period that he realized he could not marry Edwina, and as she kept pressing for financial security, he put her name as collaborator on the lyric of "Along the Santa Fe Trail." Al also tried unsuccessfully at this time to convince publishers that Edwina was his permanent collaborator and he wanted her to share in his royalties. A disgusted and unbelieving publisher asked for proof and wanted to see what the lady had written. What had she published? Al, of course, could not answer such realistic questions and he stopped trying.

Al eventually asked Edwina to sign a release with Warners, for an undisclosed sum of money, revoking all interest in the song "Along the Santa Fe Trail," though her name still appears on the sheet music.

Trying unsucessfully to land another job in New York, Al shuttled back and forth between New York and Hollywood, accompanied by Edwina and her mother. But still, hard pressed as he was for money and drugs, his song "Where Was I?" written with W. Frank Harling, made the Hit Parade in 1940.

In January of 1941, Al and nurse Perrin arrived at the Biltmore Hotel; Al was going to try to get a job with a studio. He had not come back to Hollywood by choice but by necessity. He had to have a steady income to support his habit and his two women. He had no contacts for drugs in Los Angeles so nurse Perrin called Dr.

Frederick Bergstrom when Al became violently ill with withdrawal. Dr. Bergstrom said he saw a "very sick man, suffering from chills, fever, diarrhea and nausea. Mr. Dubin also claimed to be in severe pain with a headache. He was obviously quite sick so I gave him an injection of morphine.

"A couple of days later, this nurse phoned me and said Mr. Dubin needed another shot of morphine. I realized then that he did not have intestinal flu but that he was an addict and his symptoms had been withdrawal symptoms. I told him I could not continue to treat him with morphine—that he needed help for his addiction. It would not be ethical of me to supply his habit."

Both Al and nurse Perrin became enraged at this statement and Mrs. Perrin turned Dr. Bergstrom into the drug authorities, claiming falsely that he had been supplying Al with drugs for years.

Dr. Bergstrom, hoping to help Al kick his habit, recommended a reputable nurse for him to help him gradually give up his drugs. Al agreed to the treatment and moved into a bungalow court at 1725 Sycamore in Hollywood, with Edwina and her mother housed just across the way from him.

By March of 1941, Al was willing to eat humble pie to obtain employment and asked Warner Brothers for a steady job. He signed a contract with them on March 12, 1941. The contract stipulated: "In the event Composer suffers or asserts any incapacity within the purview hereof, Producer shall have the right to investigate the nature and extent of such incapacity by its own physician or otherwise, and Composer agrees to lend his assistance to any such investigation and agrees to submit

to any and all physical examinations requested by Producer." News of his drug habit had preceded Al Dubin to California!

Al was required to report to the studio daily, to agree to allow Warner Brothers to lend his services to other producers and was to receive in payment $500 per week with the possibility of a $50 raise every six months.

The songwriter had left Hollywood a bright star; he returned a fallen one.

Al's trouble with drug addiction, with the mother-daughter duo of Edwina and Mrs. Perrin were not the end of his problems. His wife discovered he was in town and on May 1, 1941, brought suit in superior court to enforce terms of their property settlement agreement, claiming that Al Dubin had fallen behind in payments to the melancholy tune of $8,000.

I had not seen my father since I was fourteen years old and now that I was eighteen I wanted to renew our relationship. I got his address by phoning Leo Forbstein of Warners' music department. Unfortunately, Leo gave me Edwina's bungalow court number and I was shocked when Mrs. Perrin answered the door and graciously invited me in. I stared at Edwina, trying to believe she was just my age—she looked at least thirty to me.

Both of them assured me how much my father loved me and then Edwina told me she had never had anything to do with my father sexually—they were just "good friends." She told me he insisted she come to Hollywood so he could make her a "big star."

"Al is like a great fighter; he keeps hitting your vulnerable spot and I do so want to be an actress."

Mrs. Perrin told me the nurse Dr. Bergstrom had ordered was "addicting your father to drugs. She's an evil woman."

Naïvely, I believed every word. The next time I saw them, however, I was accompanied by Ed Conroy, my mother's late attorney. Edwina outrageously flirted with the man, repeatedly telling him how handsome he was and how "he didn't look old like most lawyers" and that "I'm not a bit frightened of you."

She repeated her statement that Al Dubin was a "friend" who was going to make her a star in Hollywood and intimated that she had been repeatedly "betrayed" by this "awful" man who was not keeping his promises to her and she simply did not know where all his money went. She certainly wasn't getting any of it.

I wanted an explanation. Who were these two women? Why was he refusing to send any money to my mother? Would we still share the closeness we had shared when I was a child? I finally got in touch with him and we agreed to meet at a drugstore on the corner of Franklin and Western in Hollywood.

When he walked into the drugstore and came to kiss me, I stared in disbelief. This old man just couldn't be my father. The man who had towered over me when I was a child had shrunk. We saw eye-to-eye. Though he was barely fifty years old, he looked more like sixty-five. His hair was thin and sparse, his skin loose and flabby, his green eyes dull.

It was a meeting of mutual disappointment.

He asked me if I had a boyfriend and when I replied in the affirmative, he asked me what my boyfriend did for a living and I told him Bob was a printer.

"A printer?" he asked with dismay. "I had such high hopes for you when you were a child and here you are just a printer's girl."

I wanted to respond that he had been such a terrific father to me when I was a child and that I still needed and wanted one even though I was eighteen. Out of loyalty to my mother, I tried to talk to him about money, to tell him what a difficult time she had had and how she had scrounged to keep me in college.

He replied that she had "lots of orange groves in Fullerton" and I simply could not convince him otherwise. I then tried to tell him Edwina Coolidge had said some "mean" things about him and he accused me of lying.

"Her mother said those things. She didn't."

"But, Daddy, she *did!*" I replied, very frustrated by now.

"No, she didn't." And the subject was closed.

He was much more interested in trying to sell his stock in the Del Mar Race Track for some quick cash than he was in visiting with me.

We went to a restaurant where he ordered himself a double rye on the rocks. Some of the old charm came through as he gallantly asked me what was my pleasure in the food department. But he seemed distant, faraway, as if he were listening to other voices. He was politely aloof. He was definitely not the Al Dubin of the thirties.

TEN

DURING THIS STORMY and unhappy period, Dave Franklin, a composer of popular music, who had written, as a collaborator, the very popular thirties tune, "The Merry-Go-Round Broke Down," entered Al Dubin's life. Dave had composed a lovely waltz tune for which he wanted Al to author the lyrics. The two men took off for Arrowhead Springs to work and while there, Al confided in Dave, telling him his troubles—a somewhat biased version, to be sure.

Al explained that his wife was harassing him, making it very difficult for him to work; that she was demanding money from him that he did not have; that she was extremely wealthy and didn't need his money. Franklin's sympathies were all with Al who had the misfortune to have gotten tied up with such a greedy lady.

When they returned from Arrowhead, Al and Dave went to the family home on Maple Drive to work. One afternoon, Dave let drop a remark about my mother that was untrue and I told Dave how it really was. He

didn't believe me, attributing my explanation to the fact that I was a loyal "mama's girl." It was not until later that Dave Franklin was to learn how wrong he was!

In the meantime, Edwina, unable to marry Al or to be cut in on his copyrights, decided to leave the sinking ship that was Al Dubin and she and her mama left for New York. Al had fired his nurse and now he was left to take care of his drug habit by himself.

Helen began to get calls at four or five a.m. from various hospitals and hotels.

"Come and get this man. He is causing trouble."

One such call came from a desperate clerk at a maternity hospital on La Brea. He was upsetting all the women in labor.

"But how did he get in a maternity hospital?" my mother asked.

"He was brought in on an emergency basis; he claimed he was dying with pain and we couldn't find anything wrong with him. Please come and get him. He is running up and down the halls screaming for a shot of morphine for his pain."

My mother woke me and I dutifully drove to the hospital to get my father. By the time we arrived, someone else had already collected him.

Eventually, Al found his way to the Gilbert Hotel on Cahuenga Boulevard in Hollywood. He was unshaven, sick, pleading for "a doctor to give me a shot for my migraine headache." As usual, the management called Helen, informing her that they were evicting him immediately, as they could not tolerate his running through the lobby naked. Obviously, pointed out the manager, no matter how many famous lyrics he had written, he was definitely bad for business.

"Come and get him!" was the loud and clear message.

My mother sent me to the Gilbert Hotel to stay with my father while she consulted with advisors and friends as to what to do with her estranged and sick husband. My father kept asking me to get a doctor; to call his brother Joe who would get him a doctor. I called Joe Dubin, who kindly declined to become involved in the situation.

When he was not asleep, Al became increasingly agitated and decided at one point that he was dying. My mother could handle that one! She sent for a priest from Blessed Sacrament Church. By this time, Dave Franklin and his new bride Dorothy arrived at the Gilbert Hotel to offer assistance. When the priest left his room, Al seemed calmer and Helen explained to Dave that "all Al's sins are forgiven him now." Jewish Franklin had a hard time coping with that one—not comprehending how a lifetime of sins could be wiped away in less than an hour.

After much soul-searching, my mother decided she must get help for her husband, so Dave and Dorothy Franklin and my mother and I drove the streets of Los Angeles until four a.m. looking for help. There was none. Georgia Street Receiving Hospital did not want him; private hospitals did not treat drug problems. We felt hopeless, exhausted, defeated. Something had to be done with him. But what? Finally, we were told, the police were our only recourse. Helen Dubin called the police.

Two young policemen arrived at the Gilbert Hotel in the wee small hours of the morning, ready to take Al Dubin to jail, where we thought he would receive help.

"What will you do with him," Helen asked, "when he starts screaming and carrying on like he does here at the hotel?"

"Oh, don't worry, lady, we just turn the big hoses of water on him until he shuts up."

I started to cry.

The policemen reaffirmed that "this was the only way for an addict" and "it's good for them" and "taught them a lesson" and "sobered them up".

I continued to cry.

"The man is her father," my mother told the policemen, with as much dignity as she could muster after a sleepless and frustrating night.

"Lady, you want us to take the guy or do you want to handle it?"

They were growing impatient.

"We will try to find some other way, but thank you for coming," my mother replied.

Again we had no solution.

We went home for a few hours' sleep, assuring the management at the Gilbert Hotel that we would be back later in the day. When we arrived, my father pleaded with us to take him to the nearest doctor. We got him dressed and on his wobbly legs and took him to the nearest medical building in Hollywood. On the way up the elevator, my father turned to me and said: "Patrish, I want you to know that I love you better than anyone or anything in this whole wide world."

As he was delivering this poignant message, I happened to observe, with horror, that he had neglected to close his fly.

"Daddy," I whispered, "your fly is open."

The "We're in the Money" number from *The Golddiggers of 1933*.

Warner Baxter is the harassed director for *Forty-Second Street*. George E. Stone is his assistant. Among the chorus girls are Ruby Keeler and Una Merkel on the left, Ginger Rogers on the right.

Ginger, Ruby and Una in the front line for *Forty-Second Street,*
where "Shuffle Off to Buffalo" was born.

"Pettin' in the Park" from *The Golddiggers of 1933*.

James Cagney at center stage for a scene from *Footlight Parade*. This is the one that featured "Shanghai Lil."

Joan Blondell is at center stage for the big, socially conscious production number, "Remember My Forgotten Man," from *The Golddiggers of 1933*.

A major production scene from *Moulin Rouge* (not the one about Toulouse-Lautrec) which featured "Boulevard of Broken Dreams."

Al Dubin and the author, Lake Arrowhead, 1937. This is the way she will always remember him.

Suddenly, he started to laugh, a deep belly laugh and those green eyes sparkled for a moment.

"Here I am," he said, "telling you how much I love you. This is a dramatic moment. And *you* tell me my fly is open. Oh, Patrish!" And he patted my head, laughing at the situation. He never lost his sense of humor, even in darkest moments.

The lightness of the incident broke the terrible tension my mother and I had been living under for the past seventy-two hours. We were hopeful that Dr. Bodner, a urologist, could help him with some magic emergency treatment. And when my father said the doctor looked so much like his own father, Dr. Simon Dubin, my mother thought all would soon be well.

The doctor decided Al Dubin needed a vitamin B-12 shot, but when he administered it his patient immediately lost consciousness.

The doctor's suspicions were aroused. He asked Helen if her husband was an addict.

"I don't know!" she answered in despair and confusion. "I honestly don't know. He says he isn't; he swears he isn't and it's hard not to believe him. I—just—don't know."

The urologist suggested she contact Dr. Bergstrom and Bergstrom suggested a sanitarium in Compton, the only place he knew that treated addiction.

My mother called there and was told to bring the patient to their facility and they would interview him.

It took us an hour or so to drive there. I sat in back with my gloomy father who was petulant and would have been non-cooperative if he had had the strength.

Because he was sadly and pensively staring out the car window, I tried to cheer him up by making light and meaningless conversation.

"Daddy, they will probably give you a nice room and a bath and clean p.j.'s when you get there."

He smiled.

"Patti! Wouldn't that be funny?"

"Wouldn't what be funny?" I asked, perplexed.

"Maybe that's all that's wrong with me. I need a bath." And he started to laugh.

We arrived at Dr. Geswell Burns's Compton Sanitarium at about three p.m. The nurse talked in hushed tones to my mother until she explained that I knew all about my father's problem and had witnessed, firsthand, the harrowing events of the past couple of days.

Dr. Burns agreed to take on Al Dubin as a patient and, after my mother made the financial arrangements, we left him there, hoping that he could beat whatever odds he had to beat.

When we visited Al each week at the Compton Sanitarium, he appeared restless, moody, unhappy, distant. Though I tried to interest him in some topic or other, he sat in a chair looking off into space, picking at his face and chewing tobacco. I was in Compton. I don't know where Al Dubin was.

On one visit, I tried to defend my mother when he started on his "she-took-all-my-money" routine.

"Daddy, Mother is paying for this hospital and it's very expensive and she doesn't have that much money. I think she's going to mortgage the house to meet the expenses here."

"Don't you start on me, too. You, of all people," he screamed, moving toward me with a raised arm.

I was frightened and quickly backed away from him, avoiding a blow.

Unfortunately, neither of us knew it at the time, but that was to be the last time I ever saw my father alive. I communicated with him on the phone several times after the ugly incident, but that was our final face-to-face meeting.

It was difficult for me to accept the fact that my beloved father had raised his hand in anger against me. He had done this once before when I was very young— ten or eleven years old—because I was spending my $1.00 a week allowance gambling at the Del Mar Club slot machines. Al sanctimoniously delivered a lecture on the evils of gambling.

With pre-adolescent defiance, I told him, "But, Daddy, why should you be angry? It was you who taught me how to gamble."

I made it up the stairs and into my bathroom which I locked just ahead of him. If he had been fifty pounds lighter, he would have caught me!

At the Sanitarium, Al steadfastedly refused to admit his addiction and was soon going to Dr. Burns's home (he lived on the premises) every evening for a drink or two of whiskey and to discuss writing songs with the doctor.

Whenever he got in a tight spot, Al Dubin charmed and impressed others by offering to write lyrics for their melodies. Bellboys at the hotel where he was in residence, chorus girls of his current Broadway show, bar-

bers, elevator operators, parking attendants—all were promised lyrics at one time or another. Of course, the promises were never kept after the songwriter succeeded in getting what he wanted from the other person.

One sunny Saturday morning, my mother and I drove to Compton for our weekly visit.

But the caged bird had flown the coop!

ELEVEN

THE SONGWRITER had returned to New York to be with his mistress, to search for drugs, a job and an advance against royalties from ASCAP. Though he and Edwina were back together again and Gladys Perrin was supplying him with drugs, he could not find a show. To add to his problems, Helen Dubin moved to New York temporarily to prevent him from divorcing her, and her legal separation was subsequently upheld in the New York courts. Al, furious and frustrated, was not able to divorce her.

In 1943 Al got wind of a job offering in Hollywood, working with friend Jimmy Monaco on the lyrics for *Stage Door Canteen,* a Sol Lesser Production that Columbia Pictures was to release through United Artists. His salary was to be $1,250 per week. So Al and Edwina and, of course, Gladys Perrin hopped aboard the Super Chief for California to take up residence at the Hollywood Knickerbocker Hotel. Monaco and Dubin wrote a total of twelve songs for the picture, one of which, "We

Musn't Say Goodbye," was nominated for an Academy Award. None of the other ten made the Hit Parade or were considered hits. They included: "The Alligator and the Crocodile," "American Boy," "Don't Worry Island," "Rookie and His Rhythm," "She's a Bombshell from Brooklyn" (which was a rehash of his "Latin from Manhattan"), "Sleep, Baby, Sleep (In Your Jeep)," "You're Pretty Terrific Yourself," and "We'll Meet in the Funniest Places."

Instead of writing lyrics to Monaco's tunes as he had always done in the past, Al would write a lyric and slip it under the composer's door in his room at the Knickerbocker. The songs show a definite deterioration of Al Dubin's magical talent. He had always been proud of the fact that he had a very special gift for wedding words to the music as in Victor Herbert's "Indian Summer." The expertise was not there and it must have been extremely difficult for Monaco to write melodies to Dubin's poor lyrics.

When Virginia Monaco, Jimmy's wife, came down with a severe case of pneumonia and then was quarantined with measles, Al wryly told her: "Virginia, *you* get everything your husband worries about getting." (Jimmy Monaco enjoyed a reputation of being somewhat of a hypochondriac.)

When Virginia was on the mend, she and her husband were going to have dinner with Al and Edwina and "Mama." At the last moment, Al canceled, mumbling something to the effect that, "You and Jimmy are too nice to get mixed up with people like this."

Al didn't much want to be "mixed up" with these two women by now, but Edwina pressured him constantly and on February 23, 1943, they took a limousine down

to Tijuana and went through a marriage ceremony, neglecting to notify Helen Dubin.

My father told me nothing of his Tijuana "wedding" but did call me in June to find out if I was about to graduate from college.

"Yes, Daddy, next week, on your birthday."

He was pleased that I was about to get a B.A. degree and asked for an invitation. I hedged, sensing trouble with my mother.

"If he comes, I don't!" was her adamant reply. I felt I had no choice and was left with the unpleasant task of calling to tell him he couldn't come. He was very kind. "Good luck and goodbye, baby." It was the first time he ever called me "baby" and the last time I ever heard his voice.

That was in June of 1943. On July 28, Edwina, a "bride" of five months, sued Al Dubin for divorce, charging cruelty, declining to relate detailed specifications in her complaint. Listing herself as a "stage and screen actress," Edwina asked for $175 per week alimony, $1,500 court costs and $5,000 attorney's fees.

With these two women out of his life, out of a job, alone, Al Dubin sought psychiatric help from a Dr. David Fink. Fink called Helen Dubin, saying Al was interested in reconciling with her. She told the doctor that she would like to see him "make good for a year" and then they would talk things over. Al was due to return to New York to find work.

Back in New York, Al took a room at the Empire Hotel, located just across the street from the ASCAP building. His health was failing and he turned more and more to ASCAP for advances against royalties until officers and friends of the organization made the decision

not to advance Al any more money but to take care of all his legitimate hotel, restaurant and clothing expenses as long as the bills were sent to ASCAP.

Al, riding on his reputation as a fine lyricist, managed to land an Olson and Johnson revue assignment for a production called *Laffing Room Only*. His composer was Burton Lane.

"I looked forward to working with Al Dubin with great anticipation," said Burton Lane. "I had met Dubin some years before, but I never got to know him very well. He seemed to be a very gentle man and I liked him."

Burton Lane scheduled an appointment for a Tuesday afternoon with Al Dubin to discuss the lyrics. But Al had another date—with drugs. Drugs were now the most important thing in his life. He truly had a monkey on his back. He never even gave a thought to Burton Lane as he lay on his unmade bed in the hotel.

Occasionally, Al would call on his old friend Allan Conroy, who had been a friend for years and who was very fond of the songwriter. Allan had heard that his friend Al was deeply into drugs—some of his peers referred to him as a "dope fiend"—but Allan really didn't believe it. He knew Al went to see a certain doctor a couple of times a week for injections, but Allan thought they were vitamin injections. Al always seemed to feel so much better after he left the doctor's office.

The Allan Conroy-Al Dubin relationship had started long before Al went to Hollywood. Allan was an insurance salesman and Al tried to talk his friend into coming to Hollywood and he, Al, would see to it that all his colleagues and the picture people, too, would buy insur-

ance. But Allan and his wife, New Yorkers at heart, declined.

It was to Allan's apartment that Al had brought Edwina when the romance was new and golden and (Al thought) full of promise. When he still had intentions to marry Edwina (when and if he succeeded in divorcing Helen), he wanted Allan to be his best man.

He called Burton Lane from Allan's apartment one day, after he had left his doctor's office, in good spirits. They set up another appointment, in the evening. Burton Lane was at the appointed place at the appointed time. Al Dubin was again a no-show. He slept through the appointment this time.

Finally, they did meet. Al showed Lane a title, "Feudin' and Fightin'." In subsequent appointments, Al either failed to show entirely or begged for more time to put lyrics to the title.

He never did so, and Lane wrote the lyrics himself, after Al's death, giving Al 25 percent credit because of his title. Ironically, "Feudin' and Fightin' " was number one on the Hit Parade in 1947, two years after Al's death.

Al led a very lonely life at the Empire Hotel. Edwina was out of the picture, seeing another man. Al passed his time working crossword puzzles or reading detective story magazines. He didn't even try to write a lyric. When he got hungry, which wasn't often now, he called room service. He lost weight, and he coughed a lot.

In late January of 1945, Al Dubin called Gerald Marks, composer of "All of Me." Al didn't know Marks but told him he had written several lyrics and he would

like Marks to compose melodies for them. Marks asked
Al to meet him for dinner, but Al begged off, saying he
was not well, but as an alternative they could dine at his
hotel. During the course of the evening, Al appeared
nervous, agitated. He confided to Marks that he needed
$500 immediately. Marks told Al he didn't have the
money but would get it for him if at all possible. A few
days later, Marks gave Al $500 in cash.

Al left his room at the hotel to keep an appointment
with his doctor, and the doctor wrote him a prescription
for 100 barbiturates. Al filled the prescription and
stopped at the nearest soda fountain to wash down a
large quantity of the pills with a Coke. He started back
to the Empire Hotel to keep another appointment with
Gerald Marks.

He never made it. On February 8, a beautiful sunny,
cold day, Al Dubin collapsed in the street. An ambu-
lance took him to nearby Roosevelt Hospital. Someone
called a Catholic priest and the last rites of the Catholic
church were administered to Al Dubin by Father Henry
Flautt of the Paulist Fathers Church on West 59th Street
on February 9.

Two days later, the hospital, noting the gravity of his
condition, called Gerald Marks.

"But why me? I just met the man last week," explained Marks.

The hospital spokesperson told Marks that they had
found no identification at all on Al but that they had
found Mark's phone number on a crumpled piece of
paper in Al's suit pocket.

Marks went immediately to Roosevelt Hospital where
he found Al in a coma. Not knowing that Al had already
received the last rites, Marks, who knew nothing of Al's

religious affiliation, called a Catholic priest, but the line was busy. He tried to reach a Protestant minister and was not successful. He returned to Al's room where he found a nurse taking Al's faltering pulse.

"He's almost home," she told Gerald Marks.

Marks returned to the phone in the hospital corridor and tried to get a rabbi, thinking "even if he isn't Jewish, he needs a man of God with him now." Marks struck out for the third time and came back to the dying songwriter's bedside. In a matter of minutes, the nurse said, "He's gone."

The date was February 11, 1945, the Feast of Our Lady of Lourdes to whom Al Dubin had a special devotion. Mary was the kind, warm, loving mother he never had. Many years before, Al had visited St. Anne's Shrine in Quebec to pray for an end to his wife's headaches and when Helen reported that they were gone, he also became devoted to St. Anne, the mother of Mary.

But in spite of his Catholic devotion to Mary and Anne, arrangements were made by ASCAP to take the songwriter's remains to Riverside, a Jewish mortuary in Manhattan. Al Dubin was given a traditional Jewish washing of the body, dressed in a shroud and the casket left open so his many friends could come and say goodbye to him. Edwina arrived and shrieked and yelled dramatically and hysterically.

Gerald Marks was called upon to identify Al's body at the morgue, prior to the autopsy. Though cause of death on the death certificate was listed as pneumonia, the autopsy showed he died of barbiturate poisoning. He had played out his disaster script right to the tragic end.

After Helen recovered from the shock of hearing the news of her husband's death on Walter Winchell's pro-

gram, she called Paul Cunningham, president of ASCAP at the time, and arranged to have Al's remains brought to California for burial in the family plot. It was wartime and she was told the body had to be accompanied by someone. Helen's sister, Ethel Mooney, left her own family to make the sorrowful ride on the train with her beloved brother-in-law. Al's rosary was held on February 16 and he was buried at Holy Cross Cemetery on February 17, 1945. Johnny Mercer cried and Jimmy McHugh struggled valiantly to hold back the tears. A fine, misty rain fell as the priest intoned the final prayers at graveside.

It was so like Al Dubin that he would have both a Jewish and a Catholic farewell because, truly, he was both Jew and Catholic. It was typical of his ambivalent life that he should spend borrowed money on the drugs that killed him and receive the last rites of the Catholic Church. It was typical that Edwina would cry for him in New York and Helen would cry for him in California. Finally, the duality that was Al Dubin all came together in death.

Gerald Marks had turned on his radio when he returned to his apartment after he witnessed the death of Al Dubin. The air waves sent to him the melodic strains of the beautiful "Indian Summer." Al Dubin indeed is dead. But his lyrics, nearly forty years after his death, are still alive. He destroyed himself with his excesses and habits. But he could not destroy the part of him that gives pleasure to so many—his songs.

Al Dubin was posthumously inducted into the Songwriters Hall of Fame in 1971. In August of 1980, David Merrick produced *Forty-Second Street* on Broadway which became a smash hit and won the Tony

Award for best musical of the season. The songs were, of course, Dubin-Warren songs. *Forty-Second Street* enjoyed a four-month run in Chicago and is currently being produced at Caesar's Palace in Las Vegas.

Besides his lyrics, Al left behind his wife, Helen, and his two daughters and Gladys Perrin and Edwina.

I do not know what happened to Edwina, but Gladys Perrin killed herself by leaping off the top of the Hollywood Roosevelt Hotel. Helen Dubin lived to be 81, remaining in her Beverly Hills home that Al's songs had built until her death in June of 1969. She was buried next to Al on the anniversary of his birth—June 10.

His daughter Marie married and is the mother of two sons and has three grandchildren. Both his mother and his brother outlived him.

He would be more surprised than anybody at the success of his songs in the 1980's. He could finally say to Simon Dubin:

"Dad! I made it! I carved out a niche for myself with my songs."

He surely did!

> *I walk along the street of sorrow,*
> *The Boulevard of Broken Dreams.*
>
> *The joy that you find here, you borrow.*
> *You cannot keep it long, it seems.**

SONGS

1909

PRAIRIE ROSE (Morris Siltmitzer) M. Witmark & Sons.

SUNRAY (Charles P. Shisler) M. Witmark & Sons.

1911

OH, YOU MISTER MOON (Joe Burke) M. Witmark & Sons.

1913

A FOOL THERE WAS (George Bankhart) M. Witmark & Sons.

BACK TO THE DAYS OF AULD LANG SYNE (Unknown) M. Witmark & Sons.

I'VE FOUND THE GIRL I WANT (Unknown) M. Witmark & Sons.

MARY'S COMING HOME (Unknown) M. Witmark & Sons.

MY MIGNONETTE (Unknown) M. Witmark & Sons.

ONE LITTLE SWEET LITTLE GIRL (Unknown) M. Witmark & Sons.

UNDER THE MIDNIGHT MOON (Unknown) M. Witmark & Sons.
WHY DID YOU LEAVE ME? (Unknown) M. Witmark & Sons.
WITHIN THE LAW (Unknown) M. Witmark & Sons.

1914
GOODNIGHT LITTLE GIRL, GOODNIGHT (Rennie Cormack) Al Dubin Music Co.
HE TOOK HIS GIRL IN BATHING IN THE SUMMER TIME (Unknown) M. Witmark & Sons.
HERE'S A ROSE FOR YOU (Unknown) M. Witmark & Sons.
HOO-OO I'M WAVING AT YOU (Unknown) M. Witmark & Sons.
I'VE SENT MY WIFE TO THE COUNTRY (Unknown) M. Witmark & Sons.
I WANT YOU TO MEET MY MOTHER (Unknown) M. Witmark & Sons.
MY ROSE OF NORMANDIE (Unknown) M. Witmark & Sons.
ON THE GOOD SHIP HONEYMOON (Unknown) M. Witmark & Sons.
ON THE TRAIL OF THE HONEYMOON (Unknown) M. Witmark & Sons.

1915
THAT'S WHEN I'LL MARRY YOU (Rennie Cormack) (Clarence Gaskill) Remick Music Corp.
THE BAND PLAYED ALL THE TIME (Unknown) M. Witmark & Sons.
COME BACK TO ME (Unknown) M. Witmark & Sons.

I'VE A CABARET AT HOME (Unknown) M. Witmark
  & Sons.
MOTHER O' MINE (Unknown) M. Witmark & Sons.
MY SUNSHINE CAME ON A RAINY DAY (Un-
  known) M. Witmark & Sons.
OH, YOU BEAUTIFUL BLONDE (Unknown) M.
  Witmark & Sons.
WHEN I GET BACK TO OLD VIRGINIA (Unknown)
  M. Witmark & Sons.
YOU REMIND ME SO MUCH OF MY MOTHER (Un-
  known) M. Witmark & Sons.

1916

'TWAS ONLY AN IRISHMAN'S DREAM (Rennie
  Cormack) (John O'Brien) Al Dubin Music Co.
O'BRIEN IS TRYIN' TO LEARN TO TALK HAWAI-
  IAN (Rennie Cormack) Al Dubin Music Co.
WHEN THE REST OF THE WORLD DON'T WANT
  YOU (G. B. McConnell) M. Witmark & Sons.
YOU'RE LIKE A BEAUTIFUL SONG (Joe Burke) (J.
  E. Dempsey) Al Dubin Music Co.
THERE'S A FOOL BORN EVERY DAY (Archie
  Lloyd) Jerry Vogel Music Co., Inc.
IF YOU DON'T GET MARRIED THIS SUMMER,
  YOU WON'T GET MARRIED AT ALL (Unknown)
  M. Witmark & Sons.
IT HAPPENED EVERY NIGHT (Unknown) M.
  Witmark & Sons.
MY MOTHER, MY DAD AND MY GIRL (Unknown)
  M. Witmark & Sons.
WHEN THE REST OF THE WORLD DON'T WANT
  YOU, GO BACK TO THE FOLKS AT HOME (Un-
  known) M. Witmark & Sons.

1917

AFTER A THOUSAND YEARS (James Monaco) M. Witmark & Sons.

COME DOWN TO TONY SPAGONI'S CARARET (Clarence Gaskill) M. Witmark & Sons.

DREAM OF A SOLDIER BOY (James Monaco) M. Witmark & Sons.

HAPPY SUNDAY (Bryan Gay) M. Witmark & Sons.

LITTLE COLLEEN (DO YOU BELIEVE IN FAIRIES) (Clarence Gaskill) M. Witmark & Sons.

MACARONI JOE (G. Lyons and B. Yosco) (James Donohue) M. Witmark & Sons.

MY ITALIAN ROSE (G. Lyons and B. Yosco) M. Witmark & Sons.

MY YIDDISHA BUTTERFLY (Joe Burke) M. Witmark & Sons.

ONCE UPON A TIME (George Lynding) M. Witmark & Sons.

WHEN IT'S SUMMERTIME DOWN BY THE SEASIDE (G. B. McConnell) M. Witmark & Sons.

WHY IS CECIL SELLING SEA SHELLS BY THE BEAUTIFUL SEA (Clarence Gaskill) M. Witmark & Sons.

WILL YOU WRITE THE MELODY IF I WRITE THE WORDS TO OUR LITTLE SONG OF LOVE (Clarence Gaskill) M. Witmark & Sons.

WOULD YOU TAKE BACK THE LOVE YOU GAVE ME (Ernest R. Ball) Al Dubin Music Co.

YOUR COUNTRY NEEDS YOU NOW (Rennie Cormack & G. B. McConnell) M. Witmark & Sons.

ALL THE WORLD WILL BE JEALOUS OF ME (Ernest R. Ball) Al Dubin Music Co.

MY IRISH SONG OF SONGS (Daniel Sullivan) Al Dubin Music Co.

YOU CAN HAVE YOUR SONG & WINE, GIVE ME WOMEN FOR MINE (Murray Roth) (Walter Donaldson) M. Witmark & Sons.

1918

DADDY MINE (Al Dubin) American Piano Co. (Piano Roll) M. Witmark & Sons.

EVERYONE I LOVE LIVES DOWN IN DIXIE— (Harry De Costa) M. Witmark & Sons.

HE'S GOT THOSE BIG BLUE EYES LIKE YOU, DADDY MINE (Lew Wilson) M. Witmark & Sons.

THERE'LL BE SUNSHINE FOR YOU AND FOR SOMEONE YOU ARE WAITING FOR (James Monaco) M. Witmark & Sons.

THERE'S NO END TO MY LOVE FOR YOU (James Monaco) M. Witmark & Sons.

YOU NEVER LOOKED SO BEAUTIFUL TO ME (James Monaco) (Howard Rogers) M. Witmark & Sons.

1919

CUBA (YOU MUST BE A WONDERFUL PLACE) (Paul Cunningham) M. Witmark & Sons.

LETTERS (THAT I'M WAITING FOR) (Paul Cunningham) M. Witmark & Sons.

TIS AN IRISH GIRL I LOVE (Ernest Ball) (J. K. Brennan) M. Witmark & Sons and Ross Jungnickel, Inc.

YOU'RE ALWAYS BREAKING SOMETHING AND NOW YOU'RE BREAKING MY HEART (Fred Rath) M. Witmark & Sons and Ross Jungnickel, Inc.

YOU'RE MAKING A MISER OF ME (Ernest Ball) M. Witmark & Sons and Ross Jungnickel, Inc.

YOU KNOW WHAT I MEAN (Fred Rath) M. Witmark & Sons.

WHO'LL TAKE THE PLACE OF MARY (Clarence Gaskill) (Larry Mayo) M. Witmark & Sons.

1920

MY MOTHER'S EVENING PRAYER (Bud Green, Charlie Pierce) M. Witmark & Sons.

TRIPOLI (Irving Weill) (Paul Cunningham) M. Witmark & Sons.

JUST A WEEK FROM TODAY (Bert Rule) M. Witmark & Sons.

DOWN THE TRAIL TO HOME, SWEET HOME (Ernest Ball) M. Witmark & Sons and Ross Jungnickel, Inc.

COME BACK TO JUMBO GUMBO (Clarence Gaskill) M. Witmark & Sons.

DEENAH, MY ARGENTINE ROSE (Henry Scharr) M. Witmark & Sons.

IN THE LAND OF SCHOOL DAYS (Gus Edwards) M. Witmark & Sons.

IT ISN'T THE STYLE (Harry B. Olsen) M. Witmark & Sons.

PAJAMA BLUES (Harry B. Olsen) M. Witmark & Sons.

SOMEBODY ELSE (Harry B. Olsen) M. Witmark & Sons.

SURROUNDED BY DIXIELAND (Irving Weill) (Paul Cunningham) M. Witmark & Sons.

THEY DIDN'T THINK WE'D DO IT, BUT WE DID (Fred Rath) 77th Division Association.

OLDER THEY ARE, THE YOUNGER THEY WANT 'EM (Unknown) M. Witmark & Sons.

1921

SUNDOWN BRINGS BACK MEMORIES OF YOU (Charles Edmonds) (Paul Cunningham) M. Witmark & Sons (from "Greenwich Village Follies of 1921")

TELL ME YOUR DAYDREAMS (John Mariano & S. I. O'Dice) M. Witmark & Sons.

CROONING (William Caesar) (Herbert V. Veise) M. Witmark & Sons.

THAT'S HOW I BELIEVE IN YOU (Bert Rule) (Paul Cunningham) M. Witmark & Sons.

WHERE THERE'S A WILL, THERE'S A WAY (Earl Burtnett) (Paul Cunningham) M. Witmark & Sons.

I'LL TELL THE WORLD I MISS YOU (Clarence Gaskill) M. Witmark & Sons.

I WANT TO ROCK-A-BYE MY MAMMY (Bert Rule, Paul Cunningham) M. Witmark & Sons.

WHEN I DANCE WITH YOU IN PARADISE (Desort) M. Witmark & Sons.

WHERE WERE YOU (Floyd Reese and D. L. Snell) M. Witmark & Sons.

1922

WHEN I HEAR AN IRISHMAN SING (Earl Burtnett) M. Witmark & Sons.

JUST A GIRL THAT MEN FORGET (Fred Rath, Joe Garren) Mills Music, Inc.

HUMORESQUE (A. Dvorak) Mills Music, Inc.

YVETTE (Adorjan Otvos and E. Golden) (William G. Tracey) AGAC.

WHEN THE SUMMER BIDS THE ROSE GOODBYE (Joseph J. Garren) (Fred Rath) Mills Music, Inc.

I'VE GOT FRIENDS (Joseph J. Garren) (Fred Rath) Mills Music, Inc.

1923

BROADWAY (Joe Garren) (Fred Rath) Mills Music, Inc.

IT'S A MAN EVERY TIME, IT'S A MAN (Jimmy McHugh, I. Dash) Mills Music, Inc.

HER SIDE OF THE STORY (Jimmy McHugh & Joe Burke) Mills Music, Inc.

UNHAPPY (Joe Burke) (William Tracey) Mills Music, Inc.

DANCIN' DAN (Jack Stanley) (William G. Tracey) Bourne, Inc. and Fred Fisher Music Co., Inc.

CHATTACHOOCHEE (Sammy Fain) (Billy Rose) Mills Music, Inc. & AGAC.

1924

IT'S YOUNG AND IT DOESN'T KNOW (Ch. Borel Clerc) Mills Music, Inc.

JUANITA (Leo Edwards) Mills Music, Inc.

I LOST A WONDERFUL PAL WHEN I LOST YOU (Irwin Dash) (J. Mittenhal) Mills Music, Inc.

CIELITO LINDO (BEAUTIFUL HEAVEN) (C. Fernandez) Mills Music, Inc.

O SOLE MIO (JUST LIKE THE SUNRISE) (E. Di Capua) Mills Music, Inc.

LA GOLONDRINA (N. Sarrendell) Mills Music, Inc.

A SONG OF INDIA (Rimsky-Korsakov) Mills Music, Inc.

SOUVENIR (FAIR AS A DAY IN MAY) (F. H. Klickman) Mills Music Inc.

ELEGIE (F. H. Klickman) Mills Music, Inc.

YOU CAN'T BLAME YOUR UNCLE SAMMY, IT'S
THE COMPANY THAT HE'S BEEN IN (Jimmy
McHugh, Irwin Dash) Belwyn-Mills, Inc.

WHAT HAS BECOME OF HINKY DINKY PARLAY
VOO (Jimmy McHugh, Irwin Dash) Mills Music, Inc.
and AGAC.

HARD-BOILED ROSE (Jimmy McHugh, Irwin Dash)
Mills Music, Inc. and AGAC.

SKIN-A-MA-RINK-A-RINK-A-REE (Jimmy McHugh)
(Irving Mills) Mills Music, Inc. and AGAC.

MY KID (Jimmy McHugh, Irwin Dash) Mills Music,
Inc. and AGAC.

I DON'T CARE WHAT YOU USED TO BE, I KNOW
WHAT YOU ARE TODAY (Jimmy McHugh) Mills
Music, Inc. and AGAC.

WORDS (Otis Spencer) (Al Tucker) Mills Music, Inc.

THE OLD BRASS RAIL (Abner Silver) Mills Music,
Inc.

WHEN DO YOU SUPPOSE (Rex Confrey) Mills Music,
Inc.

BETWEEN THE DANCES (Jimmy McHugh) (G. B.
McConnell) Mills Music, Inc.

I HEAR YOU CALLING, PAL OF MINE (Jimmy
McHugh, Max Kortlander) Mills Music, Inc. and
AGAC.

FOR THE SAKE OF THE BABY AT HOME (F. H.
Klickman) Mills Music, Inc.

FIRST LOVE (Frank Lebar, F. H. Klickman) Mills Music, Inc.

TWINKLE, LITTLE LUCKY STAR (A. Conover, Ed
Smalle) Mills Music, Inc.

WHAT IS THE USE (Nat Goldstein) Mills Music, Inc.

TAMARA TANGO (R. Mazziotto) Mills Music, Inc.

LOVE IS BLIND (Fred Lowe) Mills Music, Inc.

THE KISS YOU LEFT BEHIND (Gaston Gaboroche) Mills Music, Inc.

OUT OF THE PAST (Elmer Schoebel, Billy Meyers) Mills Music, Inc. & Edwin H. Morris & Co., Inc.

YOU KNOW ME AL, YOU KNOW ME ED (Ed Gallagher, James McHugh) Mills Music, Inc.

PLAYIN' ROUND (Evelyn T. Laurent) Mills Music, Inc.

NAUGHTY GIRL (Harold Leonard) (W. H. Fett) Mills Music, Inc.

1925

NOBODY KNOWS WHAT A RED-HEADED MAMMA CAN DO (Irving Mills, Sammy Fain) Mills Music, Inc. & AGAC.

SO THAT'S THE KIND OF A GIRL YOU ARE (Joe Burke) (Billy Rose) Bourne Co.

WASTED YEARS (G. B. McConnell) Mills Music, Inc.

CROSS WORDS, WHY WERE THEY SPOKEN (Clarence Gaskill and F. H. Klickman) Mills Music, Inc.

BANANA OIL (Jimmy McHugh and Milt Gross) Mills Music, Inc.

BRYAN BELIEVED IN HEAVEN, THAT'S WHY HE'S IN HEAVEN TONIGHT (F. H. Klickman) (Willie Raskin) Mills Music, Inc.

THE LONESOMEST GIRL IN TOWN (Jimmy McHugh and Irving Mills) Mills Music, Inc.

WATERS OF THE PERKIOMEN (F. H. Klickman) Mills Music, Inc.

A CUP OF COFFEE, A SANDWICH AND YOU (Joseph Meyer) (Billy Rose) (from "Charlot's Revue") Harms, Inc.

TOO MANY KISSES IN THE SUMMER BRING TOO MANY TEARS IN THE FALL (Harry Warren) (Billy Rose) Shapiro, Bernstein & Co., Inc.

MY HOME (Sam Coslow) (Irving Mills) Mills Music, Inc.

YOU'RE JUST A SHOW-OFF (James Sindelar, Andy Sindelar) Mills Music, Inc.

1926

NO WONDER SHE'S A BLUSHING BRIDE (Cliff Edwards and Irving Mills) Mills Music, Inc.

MAYBE YES, MAYBE NO, WHO CAN TELL (Sammy Fain) (Irving Kahal) Mills Music, Inc.

SOME SWEET TOMORROW (F. H. Klickman) Mills Music, Inc.

MY DREAM OF THE BIG PARADE (Jimmy McHugh) Mills Music, Inc.

WHEN A KID WHO COMES FROM THE EAST SIDE FOUND A SWEET SOCIETY ROSE (Jimmy McHugh) Mills Music, Inc.

SO IS YOUR OLD LADY (Joe Burke) Mills Music Co., and Joe Burke Music Co.

IF YOU CAN'T TELL THE WORLD SHE'S A GOOD LITTLE GIRL, JUST SAY NOTHING AT ALL (Sammy Fain) (Irving Kahal) Mills Music Co. & Irving Kahal Music Co., Inc.

I WISH I WAS IN PRISON (Sammy Fain) Mills Music Co., Inc.

A PARLOR, A SOFA AND SOMEONE LIKE YOU (Sam Coslow and Irving Mills) Mills Music, Inc.

MARY HAD A LITTLE LAMB (Billy James and Joe Burke) Mills Music, Inc. and Joe Burke Music Co.

SINGING IN THE RAIN (Lee David) (Willie Raskin) Mills Music Co., Inc. and ASGAC.

1927

IN LOVE AT LAST (W. C. Polla) Mills Music, Inc.

WHEN IT'S MOONLIGHT IN BROOKLYN (Joe Burke) (Willie Raskin) Robbins Music Co. and Fred Fisher Music Co., Inc.

A SAILOR ON A NIGHT LIKE THIS (Joe Burke) (Willie Raskin) Mills Music, Inc. and Joe Burke Music Co.

IT WAS IN THE MOONLIGHT (Joe Burke) (Willie Raskin) Mills Music, Inc.

HOW COULD JACK HORNER SIT IN A CORNER (Joe Burke) (Willie Raskin) Mills Music, Inc. (from "White Lights Takes the Air")

EVERY NIGHT I BRING HER FRANKFURTER SANDWICHES (Edward G. Nelson and Harry Pease) Mills Music, Inc.

YA GONNA BE HOME TONIGHT—OH YEH— THEN I'LL BE OVER (H. Dixon, Sam Stept) Mills Music, Inc.

TELL YOUR TROUBLES ALL GOODBYE (G. B. McConnell) (Edgar Leslie) Mills Music, Inc. and Edgar Leslie, Inc.

THANKS (G. B. McConnell) (Willie Raskin) Mills Music, Inc. and Fred Fisher Music Co., Inc.

WE AMERICANS (Edward G. Nelson) (Harry Pease) Stasny Music Corp.

WHEN I PLAY ON MY SPANISH GUITAR (Alex Marr) Edwin H. Morris & Co., Inc.

FROM SATURDAY NIGHT TILL MONDAY MORNING (Alex Marr) Edwin H. Morris & Co., Inc.

I'LL SAY I DO (Alex Marr) Edwin H. Morris & Co., Inc.

SHOW ME THAT KIND OF A GIRL (Alex Marr) (Bobby Heath) Edwin H. Morris & Co., Inc.

EVERYTHING IS SPANISH NOW (Roy Bergere) Mills Music, Inc.

I HAVEN'T TOLD HER, SHE HASN'T TOLD ME (Sammy Fain) (Irving Kahal) Mills Music, Inc. and Irving Kahal Music Corp.

AN EYEFUL OF YOU (J. Fred Coots) E. B. Marks Music Corp. (from "White Lights").

I'LL KEEP ON DREAMING OF YOU (J. Fred Coots & Walter S. Rode) E. B. Marks Music Co. (from "White Lights").

DON'T THROW ME DOWN (J. Fred Coots) E. B. Marks Music Corp. (from "White Lights").

ROLLING AROUND IN ROSES (Joe Burke) (Willie Raskin) Mills Music, Inc.

DAUGHTER OF SWEET ADELINE (Ted Snyder) (Willie Raskin) Mills Music, Inc.

THAT'S WHAT I CALL LOVE (Ted Snyder) (Willie Raskin) Mills Music, Inc. and AGAC.

SHE'S CRAZY OVER ME (Joe Burke) (Willie Raskin) Mills Music, Inc.

AFTER I TOOK YOU INTO MY HEART, YOU TOOK THE HEART OUT OF ME (George McConnell) (Jean Herbert) Mills Music, Inc.

PRETTY LITTLE THING (Henry Tobias) (Billy Rose) Mills Music, Inc.

BESIDE AN INDIAN WIGWAM (Phil Boutelje & Dan Russo) Mills Music, Inc.

HAM & EGGS IN THE MORNING (Con Conrad and Abner Silver) Harms, Inc. (from *Take the Air*).

I LOVE TO CATCH BRASS RINGS (Con Conrad & Abner Silver) Bourne Music Co.

FOLLOWING YOU AROUND (Roger Wolfe Kahn) Mills Music, Inc. and AGAC.

ALL BY MY OWNSOME (Roger Wolfe Kahn) Mills Music, Inc. and AGAC

EL TANGO DEL PERROQUET (Robert Wolfe Kahn) Mills Music, Inc. and AGAC.

IF I COULD GET TO PARIS IN 30 HOURS (Abner Silver) Bourne, Inc. and AGAC.

1928

JAZZ SINGER (James Monaco) Shapiro, Bernstein & Co., Inc. and James Monaco, Inc.

BLESS YOU, SISTER (J. Russel Robinson) Belwyn Mills.

LOVE AFFAIRS (J. Russel Robinson) Mills Music, Inc. and Fred Fisher Music Co., Inc.

MEMORIES OF FRANCE (J. Russel Robinson) Mills Music, Inc. and Fred Fisher Music Co., Inc.

YOU WON'T LIKE MARGIE (J. Russell Robinson) (Willie Raskin) Mills Music, Inc. and Fred Fisher Music Co., Inc.

HALFWAY TO HEAVEN (J. Russel Robinson) Mills Music, Inc. and Fred Fisher Music Co.

THE GIRL WHO BROKE MY HEART (J. Russel Robinson) Mills Music, Inc. and Fred Fisher Music Co., Inc.

THE FIRST KISS (J. Russel Robinson) Mills Music, Inc. (from *First Kiss*).

ANNE LEE (J. Russel Robinson) Mills Music, Inc. (from *First Kiss*).

THEN CAME THE DAWN (Harry Warren) Four Jays Music Co. and Gene Austin, Inc.

COME ON OUT AND INTO MY ARMS (J. Russel Robinson) Mills Music, Inc.

MONNA VANNA SWEETHEART SUBLIME (Phil Boutelje) Mills Music, Inc.

THAT'S ALL I ASK THE WORLD (Abner Silver) DeSylva, Brown & Henderson, Inc.

THE SHOW IS OVER (J. Russel Robinson) (Sam Coslow) Paramount Music Corp.

VAGABOND (Joseph Meyer) Remick Music Corp.

BETWEEN YOU AND ME AND THE FLOOR LAMP (Harry Link) Harms, Inc.

I MUST BE DREAMING (Pat Flaherty & Al Sherman) Top Notch Music Corp.

1929

BOUNCING THE BABY AROUND (Joe Burke) M. Witmark & Sons (from *She Couldn't Say No*).

IF YOUR BEST FRIEND WON'T TELL YOU (Joe Burke) M. Witmark & Sons (from *Show of Shows*).

LIFE CAN BE SO LONESOME (M. K. Jerome and Joe Burke) M. Witmark & Sons.

POISON KISS OF THAT SPANIARD (Joe Burke) M. Witmark & Sons.

WHAT'LL BECOME OF ME (J. Russel Robinson) Mills Music, Inc.

ON WITH THE DANCE (James Monaco) (Edgar Leslie) Bergman, Vocco & Conn, Inc.

LOVE WILL FIND A WAY (Joe Burke) M. Witmark & Sons (from *In the Headlines*).

PAINTING THE CLOUDS WITH SUNSHINE (Joe Burke) M. Witmark & Sons (from *Gold Diggers of Broadway*).

TIPTOE THROUGH THE TULIPS WITH ME (Joe Burke) M. Witmark & Sons (from *Gold Diggers of Broadway*).

IN A KITCHENETTE (Joe Burke) M. Witmark & Sons (from *Gold Diggers of Broadway*).

GO TO BED (Joe burke) M. Witmark & Sons (from *Gold Diggers of Broadway*).

LIKE A BREATH OF SPRINGTIME (Joe Burke) M. Witmark & Sons (from *Hearts in Exile*).

KEEPING THE WOLF FROM THE DOOR (Joe Burke) M. Witmark & Sons (from *Gold Diggers of Broadway*).

AND STILL THEY FALL IN LOVE (Joe Burke) M. Witmark & Sons (from *Gold Diggers of Broadway*).

MECHANICAL MAN (Joe Burke) M. Witmark & Sons (from *Gold Diggers of Broadway*).

SONG OF THE GOLD DIGGERS (Joe Burke) M. Witmark & Sons (from *Gold Diggers of Broadway*).

WHAT WILL I DO WITHOUT YOU (Joe Burke) M. Witmark & Sons (from *Gold Diggers of Broadway*).

DARN FOOL WOMAN LIKE ME (Joe Burke) M. Witmark & Sons (from *She Couldn't Say No*).

WATCHING MY DREAMS GO BY (Joe Burke) M. Witmark & Sons (from *She Couldn't Say No*).

AFTER BUSINESS HOURS THAT CERTAIN BUSINESS BEGINS (Joe Burke) T. B. Harms Co. and Joe Burke Music Co. (from *Sally*).

ALL I WANT TO DO-DO-DO IS DANCE (Joe Burke) T. B. Harms & Joe Burke Music Co. (from *Sally*).

SALLY (Joe Burke) T. B. Harms Co. and Joe Burke Music Co. (from *Sally*).

IF I'M DREAMING, DON'T WAKE ME TOO SOON (Joe Burke) T. B. Harms Co., and Joe Burke Music Co. (from *Sally*).

EV'RYBODY LOVES YOU (Jack Little) Publisher unknown.

TELL US WHICH ONE DO YOU LOVE (Joe Burke) DeSylva, Brown & Henderson (from *Oh Sailor Beware*).

TOO BAD I CAN'T BE GOOD (Joe Burke) DeSylva, Brown & Henderson (from *Nancy From Naples*).

COULDN'T YOU CARE FOR THAT (Joe Burke) M. Witmark & Sons.

I'M ALL BURNED UP (Joe Burke) M. Witmark & Sons.

IS IT NOTHING TO YOU (Joe Burke) M. Witmark & Sons.

DANCING WITH TEARS IN MY EYES (Joe Burke) M. Witmark & Sons.

KISS WALTZ (Joe Burke) M. Witmark & Sons (from *Dancing Sweeties*).

DAUGHTER OF THE LATIN QUARTER (Josef Alexandre and Joe Burke) M. Witmark & Sons.

FOR YOU (Joe Burke) Harms, Inc.

IN MEMORY OF YOU (Joe Burke) Harms, Inc.

THE RIVER AND ME (Harry Warren) Remick Music Corp.

LEAVE A LITTLE SMILE (Joe Burke) DeSylva, Brown & Henderson, Inc. & Joe Burke Music Co. (from *Oh Sailor Beware*).

HIGHWAY TO HEAVEN (Joe Burke) DeSylva, Brown & Henderson Inc. & Joe Burke Music Co. (from *Oh Sailor Beware*).

WHEN LOVE COMES IN THE MOONLIGHT (Joe Burke) DeSylva, Brown & Henderson, Inc. & Joe Burke Music Co. (from *Oh Sailor Beware*).

LOOKING FOR THE LOVELIGHT IN THE DARK (Joe Burke) Harms, Inc. (from *Top Speed*).

KNOCK KNEES (Joe Burke) Harms, Inc. (from *Top Speed*).

AS LONG AS I HAVE YOU AND YOU HAVE ME (Joe Burke) Harms, Inc. (from *Top Speed*).

ISN'T THIS A COCK-EYED WORLD (Joe Burke) DeSylva, Brown & Henderson, Inc. (from *Hold Everything*).

WHEN LITTLE RED ROSES GET THE BLUES FOR YOU (Joe Burke) DeSylva, Brown & Henderson (from *Hold Everything*).

SING A LITTLE THEME SONG (Joe Burke) DeSylva, Brown & Henderson (from *Hold Everything*).

THE GIRLS WE REMEMBER (Joe Burke) DeSylva, Brown & Henderson (from *Hold Everything*).

I'M SCREWY OVER LOOEY (Joe Burke) DeSylva, Brown & Henderson (from *Hold Everything*).

TAKE IT ON THE CHIN (Joe Burke) DeSylva, Brown & Henderson (from *Hold Everything*).

PHYSICALLY FIT (Joe Burke) DeSylva, Brown & Henderson (from *Hold Everything*).

LITTLE CAVALIER (M. K. Jerome) M. Witmark & Sons (from *Evidence*).

YOUR LOVE IS ALL THAT I CRAVE (Perry Bradford and J. Johnson) M. Witmark & Sons (from *Show of Shows*).

1930

MYSTERY OF CLOTHES (Joe Burke) M. Witmark & Sons (from *Life of the Party*).

YOU OUGHT TO SEE THE HORSE (Joe Burke) M. Witmark & Sons (from *Life of the Party*).

HE GOT A POISON IVY INSTEAD OF A CLINGING VINE (Joe Burke) M. Witmark & Sons (from *Life of the Party*).

IF I WERE A TRAVELLING SALESMAN (Joe Burke) J. Witmark & Sons (from *The Cuckoos*).

1931

WHEN YOU WERE THE BLOSSOM OF BUTTER-CUP LANE (George W. Meyer) (Al Bryan) M. Witmark & Sons.

CAN'T YOU READ BETWEEN THE LINES (George M. Meyer) (Pearl Fain) Remick Music Corp.

TO HAVE AND HOLD YOU IN MY ARMS (Joe Burke) Remick Music Corp. and Joe Burke Music Co.

WHERE WERE YOU LAST NIGHT (Harry Woods) M. Witmark & Sons.

MANY HAPPY RETURNS OF THE DAY (Joe Burke) M. Witmark & Sons and Joe Burke Music Co.

CROSBY, COLUMBO AND VALLEE (Joe Burke) M. Witmark & Sons and Joe Burke Music Co.

PAGAN MOON (Joe Burke and Al Bryan) M. Witmark & Sons and Joe Burke Music Co.

THIS IS MY LOVE SONG (Joe Burke) M. Witmark & Sons and Joe Burke Music Co.

WHEN THE REST OF THE CROWD GOES HOME I ALWAYS GO HOME ALONE (Joe Burke) M. Witmark & Sons and Joe Burke Music Co.

MY TEMPTATION (American lyric by Al Dubin) (Henry Sullivan and Desmond Carter) Chappell & Co., Inc.

IF I HAVE TO GO ON WITHOUT YOU (Harry Woods) M. Witmark & Sons.

IN A SILLY LITTLE HILLY BILLY TOWN (Joe Burke) M. Witmark & Sons.

ONLY A VOICE ON THE AIR (Russ Columbo) M. Witmark & Sons.

BECAUSE OF YOU (Walter Jurmann) Harms, Inc. (from *Her Majesty Love*).

THOUGH YOU'RE NOT THE FIRST ONE (Walter Jurmann) Harms, Inc. (from *Her Majesty Love*).

IF YOU SHOULD EVER NEED ME (Joe Burke) DeSylva, Brown & Henderson, Inc. and Joe Burke Music Co.

DAILY BREAD (Pierre Norman & Joseph P. Connor) (James F. Hanley) Famous Music Corp. (from *Daily Bread*).

1932

LIKE AN OLD FORGOTTEN REFRAIN (Cliff Friend) M. Witmark & Sons.

TOO MANY TEARS (Harry Warren) M. Witmark & Sons.

DON'T BE AFRAID OF LOVE (Wilhelm Grosz) Remick Music Corp.

FROM ONE PAIR OF ARMS TO ANOTHER (Sammy Fain and Irving Kahal) Remick Music Corp.

COLLEGE LOVE (Ted Fiorito) M. Witmark & Sons.

HOW CAN YOU SAY NO WHEN ALL THE WORLD IS SAYING YES (Joe Burke) (Irving Kahal) M.

Witmark & Sons and Joe Burke Music Co. (from *Blessed Event*).

I FOUND MY ROMANCE FOR TEN CENTS A DANCE (Sam H. Stept) (Irving Kahal) Remick Music Corp.

THREE'S A CROWD (Harry Warren) (Irving Kahal) M. Witmark & Sons (from *Crooner*).

FORTY-SECOND STREET (Harry Warren) M. Witmark & Sons (from *Forty-Second Street*).

SHUFFLE OFF TO BUFFALO (Harry Warren) M. Witmark & Sons (from *Forty-Second Street*).

YOUNG AND HEALTHY (Harry Warren) M. Witmark & Sons (from *Forty-Second Street*).

IT MUST BE JUNE (Harry Warren) M. Witmark & Sons (from *Forty-Second Street*).

YOU'RE GETTING TO BE A HABIT WITH ME (Harry Warren) M. Witmark & Sons (from *Forty-Second Street*).

LIVING OLD MEMORIES OVER AGAIN (Cliff Friend) DeSylva, Brown & Henderson, Inc.

1933

THERE'S A NEW MOON OVER MY SHOULDER AND A BEAUTIFUL GIRL IN MY ARMS (Sammy Fain) (Joe Goodwin) Leo Feist, Inc.

HONEYMOON HOTEL (Harry Warren) M. Witmark & Sons (from *Footlight Parade*).

SHANGHAI LIL (Harry Warren) M. Witmark & Sons (from *Footlight Parade*).

PUT A TAX ON LOVE (Harry Warren & L. Wolfe Gilbert) M. Witmark & Sons (from *Roman Scandals*).

ROME WASN'T BUILT IN A DAY (Harry Warren) M. Witmark & Sons (from *Roman Scandals*).

KEEP YOUNG AND BEAUTIFUL (Harry Warren) M. Witmark & Sons (from *Roman Scandals*).

NO MORE LOVE (Harry Warren) M. Witmark & Sons (from *Roman Scandals*).

BUILD A LITTLE HOME (Harry Warren) M. Witmark & Sons (from *Roman Scandals*).

SHADOW WALTZ (Harry Warren) Remick Music Corp. (from *Gold Diggers of 1933*).

WE'RE IN THE MONEY (Harry Warren) Remick Music Corp. (from *Gold Diggers of 1933*).

PETTIN' IN THE PARK (Harry Warren) Remick Music Corp. (from *Gold Diggers of 1933*).

REMEMBER MY FORGOTTEN MAN (Harry Warren) Remick Music Corp. (from *Gold Diggers of 1933*).

I'VE GOT TO SING A TORCH SONG (Harry Warren) Remick Music Corp. (from *Gold Diggers of 1933*).

1934

SONG OF SURRENDER (Harry Warren) Remick Music Corp. (from *Moulin Rouge*).

THE BOULEVARD OF BROKEN DREAMS (Harry Warren) Remick Music Corp. (from *Moulin Rouge*).

COFFEE IN THE MORNING, KISSES AT NIGHT (Harry Warren) Remick Music Corp. (from *Moulin Rouge*).

DON'T SAY GOODNIGHT (Harry Warren) M. Witmark & Sons (from *Wonder Bar*).

WHY DO I DREAM THOSE DREAMS (Harry Warren) M. Witmark & Sons (from *Wonder Bar*).

VIVA LA FRANCE (Harry Warren) M. Witmark & Sons (from *Wonder Bar*).

WONDER BAR (Harry Warren) M. Witmark & Sons (from *Wonder Bar*).

GOIN' TO HEAVEN ON A MULE (Harry Warren) M. Witmark & Sons (from *Wonder Bar*).

I ONLY HAVE EYES FOR YOU (Harry Warren) Remick Music Corp. (from *Dames*).

DAMES (Harry Warren) Remick Music Corp. (from *Dames*).

THE GIRL AT THE IRONING BOARD (Harry Warren) Remick Music Corp. (from *Dames*).

I'LL STRING ALONG WITH YOU (Harry Warren) M. Witmark & Sons (from *Twenty Million Sweethearts*).

FAIR AND WARMER (Harry Warren) M. Witmark & Sons (from *Twenty Million Sweethearts*).

WHAT ARE YOUR INTENTIONS (Harry Warren) M. Witmark & Sons (from *Twenty Million Sweethearts*).

OUT FOR NO GOOD (Harry Warren) M. Witmark & Sons (from *Twenty Million Sweethearts*).

SWEET MUSIC (Harry Warren) M. Witmark & Sons (from *Sweet Music*).

1935

CASINO DE PAREE (Harry Warren) M. Witmark & Sons (from *Go Into Your Dance*).

A GOOD OLD FASHIONED COCKTAIL WITH A GOOD OLD FASHIONED GIRL (Harry Warren) M. Witmark & Sons (from *Go Into Your Dance*).

SPAIN (Harry Warren) M. Witmark & Sons (from *Go Into Your Dance*).

GO INTO YOUR DANCE (Harry Warren) M. Witmark & Sons (from *Go Into Your Dance*).

ABOUT A QUARTER TO NINE (Harry Warren) M. Witmark & Sons (from *Go Into Your Dance*).

MAMMY, I'LL SING ABOUT YOU (Harry Warren) M. Witmark & Sons (from *Go Into Your Dance*).

SHE'S A LATIN FROM MANHATTAN (Harry Warren) M. Witmark & Sons (from *Go Into Your Dance*).

THE LITTLE THINGS YOU USED TO DO (Harry Warren) M. Witmark & Sons (from *Go Into Your Dance*).

THE WORDS ARE IN MY HEART (Harry Warren) M. Witmark & Sons (from *Gold Diggers of 1935*).

LULLABY OF BROADWAY (Harry Warren) M. Witmark & Sons (from *Gold Diggers of 1935*).

I'M GOIN' SHOPPIN' WITH YOU (Harry Warren) M. Witmark & Sons (from *Gold Diggers of 1935*).

LONELY GONDOLIER (Harry Warren) M. Witmark & Sons (from *Broadway Gondolier*).

THE PIG AND THE COW AND THE DOG AND THE CAT (Harry Warren) M. Witmark & Sons (from *Broadway Gondolier*).

FLAGENHEIM'S ODORLESS CHEESE (Harry Warren) M. Witmark & Sons (from *Broadway Gondolier*).

LULU'S BACK IN TOWN (Harry Warren) M. Witmark & Sons (from *Broadway Gondolier*).

OUTSIDE OF YOU (Harry Warren) M. Witmark & Sons (from *Broadway Gondolier*).

THE ROSE IN HER HAIR (Harry Warren) M. Witmark & Sons (from *Broadway Gondolier*).

YOU CAN BE KISSED (Harry Warren) M. Witmark & Sons (from *Broadway Gondolier*).

SWEET AND SLOW (Harry Warren) Remick Music Corp. (from *Broadway Gondolier*).

BROADWAY CINDERELLA (Harry Warren) Harms, Inc. (from *Stars Over Broadway*).

YOU LET ME DOWN (Harry Warren) Harms, Inc. (from *Stars Over Broadway*).

WHERE AM I (Harry Warren) Harms, Inc. (from *Stars Over Broadway*).

AT YOUR SERVICE MADAME (Harry Warren) Harms, Inc. (from *Stars Over Broadway*).

BROWNSTONE BABY (Harry Warren) Harms, Inc. (from *Stars Over Broadway*).

I'D RATHER LISTEN TO YOUR EYES (Harry Warren) Remick Music Corp. (from *Shipmates Forever*).

DON'T GIVE UP THE SHIP (Harry Warren) Remick Music Corp. (from *Shipmates Forever*).

I'D LOVE TO TAKE ORDERS FROM YOU (Harry Warren) Remick Music Corp. (from *Shipmates Forever*).

LIVING ON VELVET (Harry Warren) Remick Music Corp. (from *Living on Velvet*).

MUCHACHA (Harry Warren) Remick Music Corp. (from *In Caliente*).

PAGE MISS GLORY (Harry Warren) M. Witmark & Sons (from *Page Miss Glory*).

1936

FOR A BUCK AND A QUARTER A DAY (Harry Warren) M. Witmark & Sons (from *Sons o'Guns*).

HAVING A WONDERFUL TIME (WISH YOU WERE HERE) (Harry DeCosta) M. Witmark & Sons.

I'LL SING YOU A THOUSAND LOVE SONGS (Harry Warren) Remick Music Corp. (from *Cain and Mabel*).

CONEY ISLAND (Harry Warren) Remick Music Corp. (from *Cain and Mabel*).

MY SILVER DOLLAR MAN (Harry Warren) Harms, Inc. (from *Marked Woman*).

MY KINGDOM FOR A KISS (Harry Warren) M. Witmark & Sons (from *Hearts Divided*).

TWO HEARTS DIVIDED (Harry Warren) M. Witmark & Sons (from *Hearts Divided*).

I DON'T HAVE TO DREAM AGAIN (Harry Warren) M. Witmark & Sons (from *Colleen*).

AN EVENING WITH YOU (Harry Warren) M. Witmark & Sons (from *Colleen*).

BOULEVARDIER FROM THE BRONX (Harry Warren) M. Witmark & Sons (from *Colleen*).

YOU GOTTA KNOW HOW TO DANCE (Harry Warren) M. Witmark & Sons (from *Colleen*).

ALL'S FAIR IN LOVE AND WAR (Harry Warren) Harms, Inc. (from *Gold Diggers of 1937*).

WITH PLENTY OF MONEY AND YOU (Harry Warren) Harms, Inc. (from *Gold Diggers of 1937*).

SUMMER NIGHT (Harry Warren) M. Witmark & Sons (from *Sing Me a Love Song*).

THE LITTLE HOUSE THAT LOVE BUILT (Harry Warren) Remick Music Corp. (from *Sing Me a Love Song*).

THAT'S THE LEAST YOU CAN DO FOR THE LADY (Harry Warren) Remick Music Corp. (from *Sing Me a Love Song*).

1937

HOW COULD YOU? (Harry Warren) Remick Music Corp. (from *San Quentin*).

SEPTEMBER IN THE RAIN (Harry Warren) Remick Music Corp. (from *Melody for Two*).

MELODY FOR TWO (Harry Warren) Remick Music Corp. (from *Melody for Two*).

REMEMBER ME? (Harry Warren) M. Witmark & Sons (from *Mr. Dodd Takes the Air*).

AM I IN LOVE? (Harry Warren) M. Witmark & Sons (from *Mr. Dodd Takes the Air*).

HERE COMES THE SANDMAN (Harry Warren) M. Witmark & Sons (from *Mr. Dodd Takes the Air*).

THE GIRL YOU USED TO BE (Harry Warren) M. Witmark & Sons (from *Mr. Dodd Takes the Air*).

'CAUSE MY BABY SAYS IT'S SO (Harry Warren) Remick Music Corp. (from *The Singing Marine*).

I KNOW NOW (Harry Warren) Remick Music Corp. (from *The Singing Marine*).

THE LADY WHO COULDN'T BE KISSED (Harry Warren) Remick Music Corp. (from *The Singing Marine*).

YOU CAN'T RUN AWAY FROM LOVE TONIGHT (Harry Warren) Remick Music Corp. (from *The Singing Marine*).

THE SONG OF THE MARINES (Harry Warren) Remick Music Corp. (from *The Singing Marine*).

ANGEL IN A FURNISHED ROOM (Ted Fiorito) M. Witmark & Sons.

IF I WERE A LITTLE POND LILY (Harry Warren) M. Witmark & Sons. (from *Mr. Dodd Takes the Air*).

STOLEN HOLIDAY (Harry Warren) Remick Music Corp. (from *Stolen Holiday*).

1938

A STRANGER IN PAREE (Harry Warren) Remick Music Corp. (from *Gold Diggers in Paris*).

I WANNA GO BACK TO BALI (Harry Warren) Remick Music Corp. (from *Gold Diggers in Paris*).

THE LATIN QUARTER (Harry Warren) Remick Music Corp. (from *Gold Diggers in Paris*).

PUT THAT DOWN IN WRITING (Harry Warren) Remick Music Corp. (from *Gold Diggers in Paris*).

GARDEN OF THE MOON (Harry Warren) (Johnny Mercer) Harms, Inc. (from *Garden of the Moon*).

LOVE IS WHERE YOU FIND IT (Harry Warren) (Johnny Mercer) Harms, Inc. (from *Garden of the Moon*).

CONFIDENTIALLY (Harry Warren) (Johnny Mercer) Harms, Inc. (from *Garden of the Moon*).

THE GIRLFRIEND OF THE WHIRLING DERVISH (Harry Warren) (Johnny Mercer) Harms, Inc. (from *Garden of the Moon*).

THE LADY ON THE TWO-CENT STAMP (Harry Warren) (Johnny Mercer) Harms, Inc. (from *Garden of the Moon*).

YOU'RE AN EDUCATION (Harry Warren) Remick Music Corp.

YOU BETTER KEEP BABYING BABY (Jack Stanley) (William G. Tracey) Broadway Music Corp.

1939

WHERE WAS I? (W. Franke Harling) Remick Music Corp.

DANGER IN THE DARK (Jimmy McHugh) Harms, Inc. (from *Streets of Paris*).

DOIN' THE CHAMBERLAIN (Jimmy McHugh) Harms, Inc. (from *Streets of Paris*).

INDIAN SUMMER (Victor Herbert) Harms, Inc.

IN MY MEMOIRS (Jimmy McHugh) Harms, Inc. (from *Streets of Paris*).

IS IT POSSIBLE (Jimmy McHugh) Harms, Inc. (from *Streets of Paris*).

READING, WRITING AND RHYTHM (Jimmy McHugh) Harms, Inc. (from *Streets of Paris*).

RENDEZVOUS TIME IN PAREE (Jimmy McHugh) Harms, Inc. (from *Streets of Paris*).

SOUTH AMERICAN WAY (Jimmy McHugh) Harms, Inc. (from *Streets of Paris*).

WE CAN LIVE ON LOVE (Jimmy McHugh) Harms, Inc. (from *Streets of Paris*).

THREE LITTLE MAIDS (Jimmy McHugh) Harms, Inc. (from *Streets of Paris*).

ROBERT THE ROUE FROM READING, PA (Jimmy McHugh) Harms, Inc. (from *Streets of Paris*).

1940

CRAZY AS A LOON (Jimmy McHugh) DeSylva, Brown & Henderson (from *Keep Off the Grass*).

CLEAR OUT OF THIS WORLD (Jimmy McHugh) DeSylva, Brown & Henderson (from *Keep Off the Grass*).

A LATIN TUNE, A MANHATTAN MOON AND YOU (Jimmy McHugh) DeSylva, Brown & Hendersom (from *Keep Off the Grass*).

I NEVER FELT THIS WAY BEFORE (Duke Ellington) Robbins Music Corp.

ALONG THE SANTA FE TRAIL (Will Grosz) (Edwina Coolidge) Harms, Inc. (from *The Santa Fe Trail*).

1941

IT HAPPENED IN HAWAII (Mabel Wayne) Remick Music Corp.

THE ANGELS CAME THRU (Ernest Lecuona) Remick Music Corp.

THE ANNIVERSARY WALTZ (Dave Franklin) Mayfair Music Corp.

1942

A SOLDIER DREAMS OF YOU TONIGHT (Cliff Friend) M. Witmark & Sons.

I'M AFRAID OF YOU TONIGHT (Cliff Friend) Remick Music Corp.

1943

WE MUSN'T SAY GOODBYE (James Monaco) Edwin H. Morris & Co. (from *Stage Door Canteen*).

SHE'S A BOMBSHELL FROM BROOKLYN (James Monaco) Edwin H. Morris & Co. (from *Stage Door Canteen*).

A ROOKIE AND HIS RHYTHM (James Monaco) Edwin H. Morris & Co. (from *Stage Door Canteen*).

THE ALLIGATOR AND THE CROCODILE (James Monaco) Edwin H. Morris & Co. (from *Stage Door Canteen*).

AMERICAN BOY (James Monaco) Edwin H. Morris & Co. (from *Stage Door Canteen*).

DON'T WORRY ISLAND (James Monaco) Edwin H. Morris & Co. (from *Stage Door Canteen*).

SLEEP BABY SLEEP (IN YOUR JEEP) (James Monaco) Edwin H. Morris & Co. (from *Stage Door Canteen*).

YOU'RE PRETTY TERRIFIC YOURSELF (James Monaco) Edwin H. Morris & Co. (from *Stage Door Canteen*).

WE'LL MEET IN THE FUNNIEST PLACES (James Monaco) Edwin H. Morris & Co. (from *Stage Door Canteen*).

DON'T BREAK THE SPELL (Dave Franklin) Mayfair Music Corp.

PRINCE CHARMING (LeRoy Holmes) Edwin H. Morris & Co.

DO YOU (Frankie Masters & Howard Steiner) Edwin H. Morris & Co.

I GAVE YOU ALL I COULD GIVE (Morris Perlman) Mills Music, Inc.

QUICK SANDS (James Monaco) Edwin H. Morris & Co. (from *Stage Door Canteen*).

JUST DREAMIN' TILL YOU COME HOME (Cliff Friend) Remick Music Corp.

1944

FEUDIN' AND FIGHTIN' (Burton Lane) Mara-Lane Music Corp. (from *Laffing Room Only*).

GOTTA GET JOY (Burton Lane) Mara-Lane Music Corp. (from *Laffing Room Only*).

1945

THANK YOU, JOE (Pierre Norman) Mills Music, Inc.

1947

(Published posthumously) THIS IS ONE OF THOSE MOMENTS (Dave Franklin) Robert Music Corp.